Anglican Difficulties

Anglican Difficulties

A New Syllabus of Errors

EDWARD NORMAN

MOREHOUSE PUBLISHING
A Continuum imprint
www.morehousepublishing.com

Morehouse
A Continuum imprint
The Tower Building, 11 York Road, London SE1 7NX
15 East 26th Street, New York NY 10010

www.continuumbooks.com

Reprinted 2004

British Library Cataloguing-in-Publication Data
A catalogue record for this book is available from the British
Library.

ISBN 0-8192-8100-X

Typeset by Kenneth Burnley in Wirral, Cheshire
Printed and bound in Great Britain by MPG Books Ltd,
Bodmin, Cornwall

Contents

Introduction

When a building begins to collapse the materials of
which it is made are revealed. So it is with the
Church of England. In my recent study *Secularization*
(Continuum, 2002) I attempted to show that Christianity in modern England has not declined because
of assault by alien ideology or hostile public sentiment but because it had started to secularize itself. It
had begun to substitute the leading tenets of current
humanism for the Revealed doctrines and moral
teachings which had for one and a half thousand
years comprised its message in this land, and was
redefining itself in terms which identified Christianity with secular ethicism. Since the materialist
humanism of our own day is largely an unconscious
orientation of life and thought, and lacks an articulate or systematic philosophical representation, the
leaders of Anglicanism themselves – and of the other
Churches similarly afflicted – have been unaware of
just how precisely they were replacing traditional formulations of the Faith with alien substitutes. They
could, had they been more conscious of their own
received deposit of teachings, have resisted the
materialism of the age; instead they have succumbed,

and are reaping a dispiriting harvest of shriveled fruits.

In this new book I shall try to show ways in which the Church of England has, because of problems in its very nature, revealed how unprepared it is to face the ideological challenges of the times. Much of what is suggested may apply to the other Churches; but Anglicanism is almost willfully incoherent, and in its indecisiveness when confronted with differences of view or policy, and its inherent tendency to compromise, its dissolution actually offers instructive insights into decades of postponed internal judgements and shaky accommodations. This, it must be noted, is in considerable contrast to its noble past and its once steadfast adhesion to its own tradition of Christian understanding. That was, it is true, a thoroughly Protestant tradition, as reference to the teachings in the Book of Common Prayer, in the Articles of Religion, and in the Homilies, will make plain. The Church of England began to re-invent itself in the nineteenth century as a 'branch' of Catholic and Apostolic tradition: an initially unconvincing enterprise, since the bishops of the day rushed into print to deny that they were the successors of the apostles, or that their Church was other than thoroughly Protestant. The balance of the argument must be in their favour since the foundation theology of the Church of England is definitely Calvinist – compare the Articles of Religion with the Westminster Confession – and ecclesiastical practice was very unambiguously erastian. To read the episcopal *charges* of the prelates, as they laid out their case against the new

Introduction

High Church writers – *charges* conveniently published in 1845 in a collection, Bricknell's *Judgement of the Bishops upon Tractarian Theology* – is to recognize a world of ecclesiological values quite alien to modern Anglicanism. The Church of England, indeed, has an unsolved problem about its authority. At the Reformation it was cut off from universal Councils, the source of theological definition in Catholic tradition, and essential issues about the determination of doctrine were inadequately addressed. Men at the time did not perceive – how could they? – that they were setting up a body which was to last for centuries. By the nineteenth century, when a revolution in knowledge, and especially the joint revisionism implicit in historical relativism and scientific discovery, placed a strain upon traditional understandings of the Faith quite new in intensity, doctrine in the Church of England was being interpreted by the Judicial Committee of the Privy Council. In reality the remit of the Privy Council was pretty circumscribed. It could discern what the Church of England was actually supposed to teach in line with its own formularies; it had no capacity to determine doctrine as such. No one has that capacity in the Church of England. The Church remains as if frozen at the time of the Reformation; and it remained an isolated body, not in communion with any other ecclesiastical bodies. Until the requirements of colonial populations prompted its replication overseas, it had no universal Christian *consensus fidelium* to which it could appeal.

But it did not atrophy. Among its numbers, through the centuries, authentic flowers of spirituality can be seen, and sure notes of sanctity. Its past contributions to learning have been extraordinary, considering the modest size of the Church of England when set upon a world scale; its examples of pastoral service, in a society more frequently noted for quiet worldliness than for religious enthusiasm, have been nothing less than heroic. It is impossible, or nearly impossible, for anyone who has been within the Anglican fold not to feel affection for an institution whose gentle tolerance of human frailties has offered true charity of sentiment to those most in need of it. When Newman departed from the Church of England in 1845, and adhered to Catholic Christianity, he experienced excruciating sorrow at his loss: the greatest English churchman of the last two centuries perfectly exemplified that gratitude to Anglicanism which they feel who first learned the teachings of Christ through her ministrations. All along, however, there were built-in problems at the centre of Anglican ecclesiology which the rigorous English practice of erastianism for centuries obscured. Parliamentary control at the top, and the social authority exercised over the parish priests, in what was still a predominantly rural society, by the squires, rendered the Church incapable of self-reform, and incapable, even, of the most rudimentary forms of social adjustment. When it began to unfreeze, in the general religious revivalism of the nineteenth century, it began what was to turn out to be a long progression to internal incoherence. The incompatibilities locked away in the sixteenth century, taken out in the seventeenth century upheavals and then put back on the shelves, came tumbling down. What observers have since beheld is an unstable coalition of religious traditions, held together by surviving strands of erastian control, by the shared inheritance of the Book of Common Prayer, and by the disinclination of the leadership to allow discussions of fundamental – or indeed, any – principles.

The genesis of Evangelical revivalism at the end of the eighteenth century suggested no threat to the Church of England's unity, for it occurred within a general consensus about the inherent Protestantism of Anglicanism. It was possible for Methodists, for example, to continue to worship at parish churches for fifty years before they separated into a distinct denomination. But when the new High Church movement appeared, in the 1830s, the appeal to Catholic antiquity, and to the past unity of Christianity, divided the Church of England in a manner which was instantly recognized. Hence the sharpness of the rejection of Tractarianism within the erastian majority, and of the ecclesiological implications inseparable from its appeal to a Church which claimed autonomous spiritual authority. Distaste for the revival of ritualist practices – which Lord Shaftesbury referred to as 'the worship of Jupiter and Juno' – was a surface revulsion against a much more intensely felt conviction that the Church's status as a national Church made claims to a Catholic identity quite unrealistic. It is also true, as some others noticed, that the ritual observances complained of were not, anyway, authentic revivals of early Catholic uses, but Tridentine splendour re-defined in the sharp light of nineteenth-century Ultramontane extravagences. The outcome was the beginnings of disintegration. At the very time that the word 'Anglican' was coming into familiar parlance, in the middle years of the nineteenth century, the Church of England was in fact losing the semblance of unity which the name was supposed to express. Since then there has been an uninterrupted internal crisis of identity. And that is the normal condition of modern Anglicanism: a body without definition, since it sidelined its teaching authority, the Book of Common Prayer, in the second half of the twentieth century; a body uneasily held together by equivocation and paper compromise; a body, furthermore, with little idea where it is going, in the increasingly alien cultural circumstances of modern society.

The Church of England does actually have a faithfully preserved deposit of orthodox Christian doctrines – its problem is that it does not teach them. Almost everything has become internally controversial. Many liberals do not really believe in the divinity of Christ, except by some very tortured process of interpretation which would instantly have been rejected by preceding Christian generations for the best part of two thousand years. Many statements of moral theology would be met with outrage if spelled out to modern Anglicans, with their secularized ethical sense that moral judgement is something to be left to individuals. Issues like divorce or abortion or adultery are all clearly defined within Anglican teaching, but both clergy and laity today prefer to leave them as open matters – rather than face the disruptive consequences, and the demonstration of an absence of unity, which public re-statements would provoke. The Anglican way – almost the hallmark of Anglicanism – is to compose vacuous forms of words within which hugely divergent viewpoints can be accommodated. It is the promotion of expediency over principle, and is the manner in which Anglicanism is held together. But the strains are getting more diffi-cult to contain; the differences of opinion too wide to bridge. There is a refreshing clarity in the doctrinal and moral understanding of the Church in the devel-oping world, and it is from there that the *coup* against the equivocal Anglicanism of England can be expected to issue. Not much force would be needed to flatten the Church of England as a coherent religious institu-tion. It is a house of cards.

But the note of sanctity continues to resonate within its membership, as traditions of piety and faithfulness to Christianity randomly survive to produce authentic evidences of religious conviction. In this resides the true sadness of the present collapse: there are so many whose lives have been constructed around former Anglican worship, and who have trusted the leadership to preserve the Church from the corruptions of the world. Do men gather figs from thistles? The plant was once wholesome, but it was torn up some centuries ago, and in the wider perspec-tive it may be seen to have settled down upon the surface, its roots not engaged with the ground of uni-versal belief. Perhaps the present collection of crises may administer such a shock that the plant may tremble into life; perhaps, then, the fruits of spiritual-ity will abound. But there is also a possibility that

Introduction

like the Churches of Alexandria, of Damascus, and of
Constantinople, it is about to move to the social
margins, its hallowed record of Christian service
fading, if not to oblivion, into shadows.

1

Failure of leadership

❧

The leadership of the Church of England was in the past never particularly notable for qualities either of efficiency or of energy. Before the reforms of the middle years of the nineteenth century the bishops resided in London for the Season and in their territorial palaces for the other half of the year; their functions, in an institution virtually without administrative machinery, were minimal. The lower clergy were integrated with secular society, and it was the company of the local squire and the members of the bench of magistrates which they kept; the more enterprising did not reside in their parishes, but employed another priest to fulfil their duties. Cathedral dignitaries too, conventionally performed their rather modest responsibilities of office through surrogates, and since nobody was very clear what the cathedrals were for, they became simply a means of income suitable for well-connected gentlemen. In the world of learning alone can the leadership be said to have been energetic. The ancient universities were in the control of clerical dons, and despite the existence of a leisurely lifestyle, the Anglican contribution to learning was, during these centuries, considerable.

The situation is very different today. The Church of England is now bureaucratized at all levels; its synodical structure of government, and the existence of an extraordinary number of committees, require servicing; dioceses now have an administrative reality. The participation of the laity in the details of Church governance, at all levels, has assisted the provision of an ecclesiastical collectivism integrated with the clerical one. Both lower and higher clergy are required by law to reside in the place of their ministries, and both, also, have to respond to the same type of regulatory controls as affect all other institutions in the country. The emergent professionalism of public life – another nineteenth-century phenomenon – included the priesthood as a 'profession', and higher standards of attention to duty resulted. In traditional society, it was the younger sons who received a vocation to the sacred ministry; their learning and capacity for prophetic insight were not, in general, markedly developed: today educationalists will testify that the brightest of their students are more likely to be attracted to the secular welfare professions than they are to the Church. In the world of learning chairs of divinity have been secularized, departments of theology have been replaced by 'religious studies' units, and only a minority of those studying religion are Christian believers. A scrutiny of the recent increase in the numbers of students taking religious studies courses in schools, for examination qualifications, suggests that their interests are in social and moral issues, and not in Christianity or doctrinal matters. Many say, anyway, that they take the courses because they are easy options – an unhappy but credible admission.

The conditions in which the modern leadership of the Church has to operate, therefore, are very much more demanding than in the past, and should elicit much higher standards of professionalism. And that is obviously being met – up to a point – otherwise the entire Church of England would have been unable to operate in the conditions of the world as it now is. But there is a basic problem. The intellectual and professional qualities of those who now run the Church (the Church Commission office in London excepted – which is, anyway, a department of the civil service) have declined relative to secular professional life. This is, not surprisingly, always denied with vigour by the leaders themselves, and by the parochial clergy; it is recognized, however, by very many who have any dealings with them. Here are men, and increasingly, also, women, of benign intention, and doubtless of professional integrity, who do not know where they are going, and who lack the intellectual capabilities to do other than operate a kind of holding-job in the hope that better days will return.

The system that creates the leadership is opaque. The press still comment on appointments as if the Crown continues to have a decisive, or an effective, voice in the naming of bishops and dignitaries. But the formalities are no longer the substance, and have not been, presumably, since the Callaghan government introduced new conventions applicable to the appointments process a quarter of a century ago. The Prime Minister's Appointments secretary still seems to engineer preferments, but the available names from which the eventual appointee will emerge come from within the Church itself, and so, it might seem, does the actual name chosen. The waters are muddy, however; the system exists outside public scrutiny. It operates, as it happens, efficiently. There is no great pool of clerical talent which is untapped: the lacklustre appointments reflect the best that is available. What they indicate is how little talent there is around. But what the system does, also, is to choose people for office who are 'safe' – who will not become involved in controversy or rock the boat. It was always so. 'Safe' men were appointed to ecclesiastical office right through the last two centuries, and the unsafe ones who did get through the system were not the product of some daring innovation by the appointments procedure but simple errors of judgement. Anyone who questions the reality of the system comes up against a blank wall. Those who benefit from it, the safe men themselves, consider criticism as indicating the frustrated ambitions of the critics – thereby interestingly disclosing their own low personal standards by attributing them to others. The system itself remains unknown except to a very small coterie of people in Lambeth Palace. Here, evidently, the safe men are identified. Since there is no structure to monitor career development in the Church of England, the reputations of potential candidates for office derive from personal friendships or anecdotal exchange – an extravaganza of networking. How this translates into the filling of places remains a matter of speculation. But the Archbishop of Canterbury's

Appointments Secretary plainly has a major role; suffragan bishops are anyway chosen directly by the existing episcopate. The formal consultative procedure, managed by the Crown Appointments Secretary from Downing Street, canvases names which are already cleared on the safety criterion by the unknown group at Lambeth and their advisors. It must be stressed again, however, that it is not the system which is to blame for the unprepossessing leadership of the Church, despite its disagreeable secrecy and the presumably empty formality of its consultative processes, but the absence of sparkling talent to appoint. What is meant by 'talent'? In an educated age it means leaders who can address their counterparts in the secular world as intellectual equals. In a moral culture obsessed by welfare issues it requires parish priests who are as professional as the enormous secular caring industry. At a time when the frontiers of knowledge are moving forward with astonishing rapidity it means Christian scholars of the highest distinction. In ordinary wisdom and judgement it means men and women of wide experience: a major fault of existing practice, and in great contrast with the past, is that preferment now goes exclusively to former parish priests or those who have spent large slices of their ministry in Church administration. Once appointed these men conceive the entire Christian ministry in parochial terms – and that just at a time when the parish system is proving to be wholly inadequate to meet modern social needs, and when it is anyway simultaneously collapsing under financial constraints.

When in office, at all levels of the Church, the cardinal principle of what is perceived to be leadership is the avoidance of controversy. Hence the perpetual pursuit of 'safe' appointments. Few of the leaders, the bishops and deans of cathedrals, are accustomed to principled action: their immediate response to the almost daily encounter with division of opinion is to support some kind of verbal accommodation in the hope that the problem at issue will go away. Forms of words are devised in order to prevent ideological confrontation; expediency is inevitably deemed preferable to principle. This pragmatism, it is true, is widely esteemed in English public life, but it is less than satisfactory in many dimensions of service, and in the case of those entrusted with the custody of religious tradition it can, and does, have disastrous consequences. All truth proceeds through the testing of propositions, and inevitably some contentions, and those who advance them, have to be rejected. As with all ages, in reality, this is a time when religious truth – doctrine – and the institution which transmits it – the Church – have to be permanently involved in re-statement of the Faith and the re-configuration of its institutional conveyance. It is, plainly, a time of extraordinarily rapid change in the culture generally. This means that the confrontation of truth and error is especially acute and frequent; the need for loyalty to doctrinal formulations especially necessary. The posture of 'middle-ground' solutions, and the acceptance of perpetual compromise as a way of institutional life, is unavoidably antipathetic to clarity and intellectual advance in the presentation of religious propositions. Every disagreement, in seemingly every board or committee of the Church of England, proceeds by avoidance of principled debate. Ordinary moral cowardice is represented as wise judgement; equivocation and economy in the construction of compromise formulae is second nature to leaders who attain their positions in the Church by the avoidance of ideological coherence. They perceive their inclinations to represent the preservation of unity, but with each fudge the institution supposedly being preserved stands for less and less. When a bishop is presented with some controversial matter for his judgement or action his immediate impulse appears to be a desire to avoid personal involvement as much as possible. Where it is not possible, a form of words suffices – and when that fails the matter is referred, rather handily, to one of the now numerous advisory committees, or even to the diocesan synod. At the national level the bishops and their advisors behave collectively in the same manner. It is usual for the Church to set up bodies of enquiry, of various sorts, to devise courses of action when a matter evoking division of opinion comes before them, using the synodical structure of government as the authority. Quite frequently their reports produce no single recommendation, but a range of possible courses of action, expressed in terms of questions. Anyone who reads the papers the General Synod has produced in the last thirty years will see at once how the inclination to avoid principled decisions operates. One result is that very little actually gets done – decisions take years to reach. Those which most blatantly avoid ideological precision are the ones that usually get through first.

The culture of expediency is so intensely expressed in the procedures of the Church of England, and in the behaviour of its senior officers, that it is how even those far removed from ecclesiastical knowledge judge Anglicanism. The press see it as the Church in which you don't have to believe anything. The bishops and deans themselves have a greater eye to their career reputations than they have to the furtherance of doctrinal purity or consistency in the conduct of the Church's affairs. They seek a smooth passage through the rocks of controversy, on which their reputations must not be allowed to wreck. These inclinations are endemic in Anglican governance: the first and greatest commandment is to get out from under – to avoid controversial decisions. Forms of words as the solution to situations of genuine ideological division are risky, however. They are liable to prove very short-lived, since the controversial issues which prompted them change all the time. Suddenly the leaders' clever solutions become a bed of nails, as the terms of reference in wider debate alter. But the leaders are at least extremely adaptable, and unblinkingly accept wide discrepancies and inconsistencies in the Church's public declarations, over the years, as apparently an acceptable condition of things. Better incoherence, they seem to say, than an internal row. Thus their adhesion to 'political correctness', many of whose new sacral values are clearly at variance with Christian teaching – particularly in relation to current sexual customs – and frequently

place them in situations where their tolerant liberalism posits a mismatch with traditional Church
teaching. Then they keep silent, evidently fearful of
any controversial denial of public practices, or of
the supposedly enlightened convictions of secular
pundits. The ruling over homosexuality represents
these processes clearly, the production of absurd
idiosyncrasies: homosexual practice was declared
acceptable in the laity but not among the clergy. Only
the Church of England could have allowed itself to get
into such a mess. An institution which declares little
becomes little, and leaders whose first instinct is to
protect their career interests will find themselves
presiding over a body which has less and less consequence.

The Evangelicals are an enigma in all this. In
reality they are internally divided over many issues,
and do not form a coherent single entity in Church
polity. Their strength indicates the relative numerical
decline of the other sections within Anglicanism, and
does not appear to rest upon a stable or definable
basis. Their period of influence may endure for a
short time, until the greater collapse of the entire
Church prompts their realignment with non-Anglican
Evangelical denominations – or what is left of them.
The Evangelical leaders are not exactly noted for
intellectual accomplishment, it is true, but when a
movement approaches ascendancy in an institution
it is to be expected that it will attract to itself all
those seeking patronage, advancement, influence,
and generally a place in the sun. But the intellectual
part of Anglicanism is predominantly liberal, both in

theology and in morals. Their distaste for the intellectual crudity of traditional Evangelicalism is only just beginning to be overcome – as the Evangelicals, now in positions of influence, are beginning to jettison a lot of their luggage and to grab the portfolios of power. The scene is actually changing quite quickly. The adhesion of a small number of intellectuals to the Evangelical citadel, however, is a minor feature of a larger shift: this is the acquisition by the Evangelical leadership of the arts of the Anglican compromisers. There is emerging, almost unnoticed, the usual psychology of accommodation, the triumph of expediency over principle. The Evangelicals are proving to be thorough modern Anglicans, whatever their formal commitment to Biblical conservatism and traditional morality. Discreetly, behind the twitching curtains of the Evangelical bishops' houses, the playing-pieces are being set out on the board. The game of compromise is beginning, flattering their sense of statesman-like judgement, and their desire to eschew controversial decisions. Nothing is really changed.

Leadership at less exulted levels of the Church of England's ministry displays a characteristic not so apparent among the dignitaries: low morale. The senior leaders may well be frustrated in various ways, but within the parochial clergy there are many who have lost confidence in their calling. There is no way of quantifying this, and many who will rush to deny it – especially the bishops, whose inexplicable assurances about the healthy condition of the Church become increasingly less realistic. It is also invidious to probe the minds of the clergy in order to judge what is the state of their morale. But the evidences are very plain, and surface at clerical gatherings, like deanery synods or local Chapters of the clergy, where, in the absence of the bishop, dissatisfaction sometimes erupts. Often it takes the form of overt criticism of the leadership, identified collectively; more commonly it derives from a kind of spiritual disorientation. It would be tempting to say that conditions, both of ministry and in the social context, have changed so radically since their ordination that the clergy find themselves enveloped in unfamiliarities for which their training had not prepared them. In reality, however, most of those coming forward for ordination are now in, or are approaching, middle age. They are quite familiar with the world in which their ministry is set. The older clergy, as is only to be expected, will show a high degree of social disorientation as the decades slip away, leaving their conception of their functions in the past. The more recently ordained, however, are often among the most dissatisfied with things; they sense that the training they have received is proving an inadequate guide to the realities of ministry, and that the episcopal leadership of the Church seems unprepared to plan strategies for a changed world. Episcopal vision, in that sense, would usually appear to extend no further than individual retiring ages. There are short-term fixes, modest re-arrangements of territorial ministries which leave the essential structure of parochial ministry itself virtually unquestioned. As usual, there are numerous Church committees and reports, which ask numerous questions, and then leave most

things as they are with only insignificant adjustments.

The modern clergy lack social definition. They no
longer fit, as once they did, into a recognizable professional category. The secular welfare workers and
carers have more prestige in the public's estimation,
and it is television drama about hospitals and emer-
gency services which attract public respect, not the
priest at the altar. The clergy are not really sure what
they are for. Many of the functions once considered a
clerical preserve are now performed by the laity – an
indication both of clerical shortages and of the heightened awareness of lay ministry. Except for one
sacramental function, the celebration of the Holy
Communion, lay auxiliaries can officiate in everything, and do. The very small numbers who
attend church services, or have any connection with
parochial organizations, have produced an unhappy
situation in which the incumbent has a relationship
to such a narrow section of society at large that effective contact with the people is difficult to establish.
Very modest successes get hugely exaggerated: the
reality is that the world is passing by, and in their
hearts the clergy know it. There are, it cannot be
doubted, Evangelical ministers who do not experience
this desolation; they are encouraged by the size of
their congregations, believe that the direct intervention of the Holy Spirit will save the day, and are
encouraged, as others are not, by the rhetorical
optimism of the bishops.

The Church of England exists as an assemblage of
parallel sections. There are those who accept the

priesthood of women, with their own bishops, and those who do not, with their own bishops too. There are some who reject traditionally understood Christianity outright, the liberals (and their fellow-travellers), and the declining Catholic wing, who, together with the Evangelicals, though for different reasons, adhere to orthodoxy in doctrine. There are those who define themselves through formal, and those who define themselves through informal, worship. And there are those who have quietly lost their faith, scarcely admit it even to themselves, and yet retain the habit of church attendance for reasons it would be impertinent to evaluate. This last category contains a number of clergy – how many is not knowable. But the pervasive atmosphere of sinking morale is such that it must unavoidably be calculated that quite a number have lost their faith, or at least retain it in such a residual form that it is practically useless in ministerial terms. Presumably they persist in ministry – some are not qualified for much else, and for the less efficient it can prove an easy life. In some there must be an appalling dilemma; their quiet heroism, as they carry on a vocation which has lost its point, needs recording. The liberal clergy, with all the self-confidence of the enlightened, are quite different. Their austere deconstruction of the Christian religion began by being residual, and they are buoyed up by the conviction that they are retaining people in the Faith by representing it in an intellectually credible fashion. To some extent there may be some verity in this. Liberalism in religion also has the effect of satisfying the questioning minds of the current generation, but that generation does not pass on much to its successors. Liberalism thus becomes, in effect, a transition to scepticism, and a path to religious decline. Some liberals have allowed themselves to go so far in their religious scepticism that they would do better service to the Church by leaving it altogether, rather than by occupying positions of ministry which are supposed to oblige them to teach its doctrines. The bishops are too weak to say anything like that out loud, of course, since it would prompt controversy. Nor are they inclined to raise any issue which might suggest tests by which religious orthodoxy can be identified.

Institutions need to protect themselves from their ideological adversaries, or they will be taken over by them, or be swept aside. Truth has no built-in device by which it is always recognized as truth: it requires institutional embodiment so that it may have its witnesses and teachers, and so that it may be transmitted to future generations. Truth means exact definition of propositions, just as in the modern secular world of values the definition of racism – to take a current sacral value as an example – is very precise. In religion, teachings have to be comparably exact. Hence the Church's past concern with heresy; and so, also, the reason why so much of the New Testament is concerned with identifying wrong ideas. Heresy is now an outmoded concept to many in the Church, and in secular opinion it suggests witch-hunts and extremism. Yet heresy is a reality, under whatever name it appears, and if the modern Church does not protect itself against error it will be overthrown by it. That task requires a clergy who are educated in doctrinal knowledge and who really do believe that Christianity is true. It is astonishing that it is now necessary to have to make the point at all.

2

Worship

❧

The greatest damage done by the practical abandonment of the Book of Common Prayer was not to the Church's guardianship of a great spiritual treasure but to its teaching office. The passing of the book – which is now rarely used in many parish churches – was lamented because of the beauty of its prose, the familiar cool words giving an organic structure to the lives of all those who called themselves Anglican. Its latest replacement – or, rather, replacements, since *Common Worship* comprises two volumes, approaching a thousand pages each – instantly disturbs the educated mind by the distressingly trite translations of scriptural passages, and the banal doggerel of the original exclamations and doxologies composed, one presumes, by members of the Liturgical Commission. The spiritual pain induced by resort to the horrors found on each page, however, may readily be converted into sacrificial suffering: the worshipper may actually gain virtue by persistence. The damage done by the removal of the Prayer Book is to the service it performed as *lex orandi*: to the systematic conveyance, through liturgical exercise, of Christian teaching. A spiritual life could be assembled and sustained through the annual procession of collects and readings in the Prayer Book, the entire work having been consciously constructed to present Christian beliefs in a manner susceptible to easy personal recollection whilst simultaneously linking each member of the Church in a union of devotion. In the absence of a coherent ecclesiology, the Prayer Book *was* the authority of the Church of England. Its forms of words and its teaching office is really all there is that joins present Anglicans with their predecessors. It is a link with past experience of the spiritual life and the means by which future generations may be secure in sound faith. The archaic language could easily have been rendered into current prose, whatever the loss to those already possessed of sentiments associated with the traditional cadences. The teaching of Christian doctrine through liturgy is the second purpose of all worship: the first is an offering to God. In the Prayer Book may be found an account of the Anglican understanding of Christian truth that cannot be found in a *sensus fidelium*, for Anglicans are members of a national Church – they have no access to a universal body which can interpret Christian teachings and thereby preserve them from error, and inform them in the difficult task of expressing timeless truths in the symbolism appropriate to the modern world. The Prayer Book is not just a collection of services, with some annexed articles and regulations. It is the authority, the only effective authority, for Anglican beliefs. The simplicity and relative brevity of the book, additionally, made those beliefs accessible to the minds of the learned and the simple in equal measure, so that the teachings of Christian truth readily became – as it is a matter of historical record that they indeed became, over the centuries – inseparable from popular culture.

In its place, and after thirty years of preparatory liturgical experiment (Anglicans spin out their incoherence) there appeared *Common Worship*. In theory there are now two legal prayer books in the Church of England. The Book of Common Prayer remains, but is fast falling out of use as generations change; *Common Worship* is the standard *vade mecum* of modern Anglican worship, and will be, in the next generation, what Anglicanism is recognized as being. As with the Prayer Book, it is not the language which is important, distressing – in fact excruciating – as the prose in *Common Worship* is. The problem with the new work is that it has effectively abandoned the teaching of Christian truth through liturgy. For the two large books comprise a multiplicity of forms, an extraordinarily incoherent array of interpretations. *Common Worship* represents a key concept of our day – choice. In place of single services there is enormous variation and option. There are eight versions of the words of Institution in the Eucharist; local worshippers choose the one most compatible with their understanding of Eucharistic doctrine. *Common Worship* is crafted on the assumption that in each parish or place the congregation will set up a worship committee who will select, or down-load, those bits of each service they like, restrained only by a very small number of obligatory sentences or exclamations. Evangelical argot predominates in the verbal renditions of sentiments that are otherwise just about familiar.

What this all represents is the abandonment of uniformity, and consciously so. The Church of England has knowingly departed from its only bond of union; and as the Book of Common Prayer slips away, lodged only in the fading memory of the old, and unknown to few beneath middle-age, Anglicanism will find itself cast upon the seas without a compass. Services will vary in each place, representing, as they do, selections made by congregational committees who – as support for the Church declines still further – become increasingly less acquainted with wider horizons. Instead of recognizing universal standards, the local users set their own sense of what moves them in worship as the determining principle in selection. Worship is now no longer a unifying cohesive in the Church, but is becoming, through local option, the reality of division. In many places, to put it bluntly, the congregations are simply not qualified to choose their own liturgy, and the assistance they receive from their priest is also, in view of current training programmes, likely to be rather less than informed or professional. Liturgy can hardly be a means of teaching Christian doctrines when the existing wide variations in the Church of England over interpretation of what those doctrines are is institutionalized in the manner of constructing it. This is pick-and-mix religion, and it corresponds to an ideology of individual choice which is new in the history of the Church.

Common Worship, then, may be recognized as a withdrawal of the Church of England from both institutional uniformity and the concept of a single *lex orandi*. It is also something else: a manner of devising services which are sympathetic to the modern notion, extremely widespread in the Church today, that worship exists as a kind of personal therapy. People increasingly perceive worship, and 'going to Church', as an exercise in satisfying individual need. Worship has to be beautiful, calming, to accommodate particular religious ideas harboured by the worshipper, to inspire aesthetic sensations, to evoke an atmosphere of camaraderie among those present. But none of these things are what worship is about in traditional understanding. Just as its second purpose was teaching through liturgical forms, so its first purpose was an offering to God. Worship is directed to him, and not to ourselves. It is not we who are supposed to get personal emotional benefit. It is God who is being served, and he is offered praise. This praise, it is true, is tendered in the finest manner we can devise – in music, sometimes, and in temples set up in God's honour intended to glorify his majesty. But any splendour which may accompany the circumstances of worship is for God, not for what it does for us. Religion is not therapy; it is not about the cultivation of beautiful sensations in the individual. It is about obeying God's laws. People today, however, regard worship as a dimension of emotional sensation – in an age when emotional satisfaction is regarded as something which should be available on a routine basis. Frequent entertainment through television, frequent sex through the availability of contraception and abortion, frequent eating through industrialized farming and processing techniques, frequent emotional uplift through worship – it's all the same. They have no sense of the august *demands* of God, which worship once evoked. Many of the formal words conveying divine laws still exist in *Common Worship*; its evangelical pedigree has seen to that. But they are received in a context of choice, which itself corresponds to personal inclination to devise religious ideas on a private basis. The new services are a very accommodating accompaniment, in practice, of the modern desire to arrive at an understanding of religion which is in accordance with personal needs rather than with the tradition of the Church. People sample different churches, different styles of worship, different selections made by different congregations. What they are seeking is not *Christianity*, but the nearest approximation they can find to a religion cobbled together by themselves. The materials they use for this necessarily have Christian resonances: they exist in a culture which was once Christian, and which still bears surviving remnants of its former endorsement by the governing classes. But the content of this search is personal satisfaction, not surrender to God's will. Some who are inclined to sacred theatre will discover it in the liturgical exercises of traditional Catholic practice or of the neo-symbolic acts which are now common in Evangelical worship. Those who like classic music can go to cathedrals; those who prefer less formal music will resort to the places where there are choruses and simulations of rather dated pop. Others will choose services with accentuated emotional appeal, hyped histrionics which always somehow seem to attract devotees. Increasingly few will discover churches where solemn liturgy is offered in the traditional manner – a manner which is actually, in the Church of England, only a little over a century old. Most will go nowhere.

Those who do go into church for a service, either for the first time to see what it is like, of after some years of lost habit, will find an unfamiliar scene. It is another difficulty for the Church of England that it has lost continuity in its worship, except in the minority of parishes which have persisted in adherence to the Prayer Book, and except in some cathedrals where the old offices continue alongside modern versions of the Eucharist. The implosion of membership in local parish churches makes the novelty of the *Common Worship* rites seem all the stranger to those who have not been softened up by twenty preceding years of experimentation with the liturgy. The small numbers now attending soon take on the atmosphere of a closed world – a tiny club of semi-enthusiasts, too self-conscious in their desire to extend a welcoming hand to new adherents yet also unsure of exactly what the institution of which they are custodians exits to do. Increasingly, with the decline in attendance, the congregations are unrepresentative of the society from which they are drawn. About the only thing that defines them is social class: the Church of England remains, seemingly indelibly, a middle-class institution. Though now, in most parishes, less well supported by more educated and professional class people, the Church members who attend worship are lower middle-class and easily identifiable in social class terms. Some who find the worship, and atmosphere of simulated intimacy, too embarrassing for comfort go off to the cathedrals, partly to achieve anonymity, and partly for the music. Above all, however, cathedral congregations seek formality and dignity in worship. They do not find it in all cathedrals. The congregations of cathedrals are actually static, except at Christmas and Easter, when they are swelled by lost members returning in the hope of remembering past seasonal celebrations, and also by members of other Churches, especially Roman Catholics at Christmas, who like the carols in a traditional, if slightly kitsch, setting – candles, cribs, choristers and high camp. The present levelling off of cathedral attendances, however, follows years of expansion. It's not a healthy sign. For the cathedral congregations are not, in general, composed of converts to the Faith, but are the consequences of defections from the parishes. They are those who can no longer bear the styles of worship in the local churches, and who resort to the cathedral as a lifeboat. This will almost certainly prove to be a temporary phenomenon, since it is prompted by spasms of liturgical reform. The spread of the *Alternative Service Book* in the 1980s produced the largest wave of exiles heading for the imagined dignity of cathedral worship – a translation of the respectable lower-middle class in pursuit of things as they had always known them. Interestingly, the use of *Common Worship* is producing fewer refugees – though a ripple is still discernable – and this is itself an indication of overall decline. Cathedral congregations were extremely small before the reforms of the nineteenth century, when nave services began, choirs became more professional, and the absentee clergy were obliged to return to their duties. There does not seem to be any indication that their present levels of support will decline; the Church of England appears to be dying back to them. But they are not buds, potentially new life about to revivify the plant; they are simply the resort of the respectable, in genteel enjoyment of the last twitches of life in a decayed institution. Throughout the Church of England there are 'successful' parishes, each eagerly acclaimed as the precursor of revival. Collectively, they are not great in number; individually they are like mini-cathedrals – attracting their adherents through cannibalizing other churches in their area. The attraction of the successful is the style of worship on offer. Traditional worship scoops up the remnants of the fading world of familiar Anglicanism; *Common Worship* forms attract others who select one church as more conducive to their personal tastes than another. The notion that a parish church should be supported because it is the parish church does not appear to have much vitality, and as the entire parochial structure begins to disintegrate, because the small numbers attending can no longer maintain the fabrics, the habit of choosing a new church to attend on the basis of its style of worship, rather than because it is a parish church, receives further stimulus. The ancient territorial arrangement of the

Church of England indicated its vocation as the national Church: every resident of every locality had a priest to attend to the rites and to give pastoral assistance. There are many reasons why this has broken down in the past century or two – population mobility, changes in the centres of population, the growth of religious dissent, the end of the rural union of parsons and squires, the supervening *anomie* of the cities. The modern pluralism of worship has simply added to all this: people do not choose a church to attend (where they choose one at all) for territorial reasons, but because they believe it is personally conducive to their religious inclinations.

Except for the middle-class schoolchildren and students who have been educated in public schools or in the chapels of the ancient universities, almost no one below forty years of age has any experience of Anglican Morning and Evening Prayer. The only service known to modern Anglicans is Holy Communion – now usually referred to as the Eucharist. Morning Prayer has disappeared from the consciousness of most church attendees because they are still in bed early on Sunday morning; at the time when Evening Prayer might occur they are before the television screen. The parish Eucharist is crafted as a family service, and is now typically according to selections made from *Common Worship* by the parishioners themselves. Thus a traveller visiting a number of Churches in his transit across the landscape will find that the various ejaculations, choruses, 'responsorials', and sections of prayer, show little uniformity, though they are arranged around some shared points.

In many churches the congregations now sit in concentric rows around a table, where the priest, in bright vestments, celebrates (or 'presides' at, in current usage) the holy mysteries. There is, however, nothing particularly mysterious about some of the accompanying liturgical drama – and it is these attempts at cultivating an atmosphere of informality and camaraderie which many of those unfamiliar with it all find so cringingly disagreeable.

The Eucharist, therefore, which was once such a visible and mysterious sign of unity and continuity in the Church has become a folksy rite, variously constructed, attended by a small company of like-minded enthusiasts. There is enough surviving structure to give it a recognizable form, but not enough to allow it to be uniform. What is actually shocking about the services, however, is not the manner of the re-enactment of the great expiatory offering of Christ but the casual lack of preparation by those who attend or officiate. It is the only service most Anglicans now know; it is also the most frequently attended. Only fifty years ago people attended only after prolonged contemplation of their sins and careful preparatory devotional exercises. There was fasting before receipt of the sacrament itself. The officiating priest was trained in preparatory prayers. Now this all seems to have gone, and the sacrament is received casually, without preparation by either priest or supplicant, and in circumstances more redolent of human fellowship than of the regret for sin. Very many of those receiving the sacrament seem to regard it as a token of human friendships and only secondarily as a participation in the death of Christ. Worship will always be the paramount act of the Christian, and the Holy Eucharist is its most solemn and essential expression. The Church of England will do well to instruct its members in how to prepare themselves for a union with Christ which at present they would appear to approach without too much thought.

The greatest loss from the adoption of the new services, let it be repeated, is not through the banality of the words, or the absence of a uniform structure which could make the rites sufficiently memorable to be the building blocks of personal spiritual formation, or repetitiousness, or the discontinuity of the sections containing each of the options – so that the worshipper is perpetually leafing from page to page in the enormous volumes – and not even from the numerous rubrics of instruction on how to use the services which cover every page: the loss is from the failure of *Common Worship* to supply a *lex orandi* which is accessible and universally agreed. There is one: there are several. But the teaching of doctrine may not obviously be drawn from the pages of the new services, as it can from the Book of Common Prayer, and when it is deduced from these chaotic selections it lacks uniformity or direction. The options are doubtless intended to be incorporative – to cater for all tastes in a Church which has no real unity. That is not a conclusion its authors will want to recognize; it is, nevertheless, the reality which results from upwards of two thousand pages of alternatives.

The Church of England is riddled with theological liberals. Despite the Evangelical majority which now approaches predominance in the Church it is still the influence of the liberals which is most encountered in educational and administrative circles. As the scale of everything gets smaller, due to the large overall decline of active membership, the liberals' role as the educated part the ministry appears more prominent. Evangelicalism is not sophisticated: it is a religion of emotional response and verbal repetition, which the liberals simply ignore in their continuing accommodation of the Church's teachings to the secular values of current intellectual culture. Despite all that is said to the contrary, the Evangelicals have not grown in size; they have adhesions and losses among their numbers in about equal quantities. Their strength is relative – it actually represents the decline of the other sections of Anglican practice. But the liberals have suffered real decline; this does not appear to affect their influence. There are consequences here for liturgy, and the teaching office of liturgy. Whereas the Liturgical Commission, which produced the new services, was constituted in a painful effort to balance all sections and styles in the Church, in practice it has shown an exaggerated deference to what its members regard as scholarly (i.e. liberal) opinion. Since the liberals' purchase on doctrinal precision is often extremely insecure the effects may ultimately be discerned in the multiplicity of alternatives in *Common Worship*. How can you worship a God who is known about so tentatively?

3

Ambiguous ethical teaching:
1. Social and political morality

Back in the heady days of the 1960s the Church of England was insistent that the application of Christianity required believers to be involved in the ways in which society was organized and the state was governed. The simple application of charity as a palliative to social distress was no longer perceived to be adequate; structural solutions were required – political action, that is to say. The message went out from numerous committees and boards of the General and of local synods, when they were set up in 1970. Synodical government, in fact, proved the perfect catalyst to convert the Church into a talking-shop, especially since those with the time and the inclination to take part in the new enterprise largely came, anyway, from the chattering classes and their clients. Political dimensions began to appear in very many issues, as understood by Church bodies; preparation for this had been provided by decades of social concern. Declarations of the World Council of Churches, of which the Church of England is a member, encouraged very advanced social and political critiques. The last of the anti-colonial wars were being fought, and the contemporaneous excitements of international student movements, not limited to militant disapproval of the war in Vietnam, heightened an atmosphere of political consciousness which rapidly affected the way Church spokesmen perceived things. Fearful, as ever, of being seen to be unsympathetic to youth culture, as they imagined it to be, Church of England statements on public issues began to be expressed in the rhetorical cadences of the protest movements. Subsequent reports, commissioned by the Church of England, on urban and then on rural social injustices, became works of pseudo-authority. They were, in all truth, more informed than much of the imagery of vulgar Marxism which pervaded the 'Liberation Theology' found acceptable among Anglican dignitaries. This series of attempts at radical interpretations of the Gospel – which made serious Marxists cringe – has left traces in the courses offered to those in ministerial training which still surprise by their innocence of acquaintance with the philosophical precision of real Marxist writers. Yet despite the excitements of the times, and the frequency with which it was insisted that 'structural' solutions (ie. political ones) must be found for social injustices, the Church of England distanced itself from the support or endorsement of actual political parties or philosophies. The paradox and inconsistency did not seem to worry anyone. Doubtless the ultimate motivation was not some incredibly sophisticated interpretation of the possible sterility of political philosophy but the customary Anglican disinclination to get involved with anything controversial. At any rate, the decades of political rhetoric were also the decades of no action.

The moral landscape of the Church of England today appears very different. The avoidance of any appearance of party politics is as conventional as ever, but the endorsement of 'structural solutions' has more or less vanished. Church leaders in their utterances – some made by bishops in the House of Lords – and luminaries of the Church in their writings and reports for ecclesiastical bodies, show themselves concerned with certain selected issues, usually those constituting the agenda of political correctness at the moment. Their opinions on such matters are derived from the encompassing texture of media debate: they are informed, that is to say, by secular moral authority rather than by resort to theological precept or the tradition of the Church. Most do attempt, in varying measures of crudity, to apply a religious gloss in the presentation of these opinions. Yet the nature of political society itself, and the philosophical basis of human association, remain unaddressed by modern Church leaders. Even the unconscious vulgar Marxism of thirty years ago seems to have departed from their endeavours. They seem no longer described by wrong thought but by no thought. In this, once again, they ape the culture in which they are set, apparently incapable of recognizing that they have another world to stand upon from which to judge this one. The result is a seeming acceptance of bourgeois liberal democracy, and of class social structures. They have ceased to be critics of neo-capitalism, and of the social mechanics of materialism. They are as close in the acceptance of existing political values as their predecessors were who, in their day, identified first feudalism and then divine right monarchy, as exemplifications of Christianity applied to world order.

The philosophical incoherence of political liberalism in our day provides the explanation. It is now often said that Western societies have recently witnessed the 'death of ideology', and in a sense this is true. Yet ideology is in fact still alive – and it is to be looked for in the various polities and posturings of the politically correct, and in militant American and British attempts to impose their own understanding of liberal democracy in the occupied countries of Kosovo, Afghanistan, and Iraq. But in their conduct of government, Western liberal states show a definite shift from ideology to management, and the nineteenth-century inheritance of bourgeois individual liberty is being replaced by bureaucratized collectivism. The State is no longer understood to promote 'higher ideals' derived from religious or philosophical systems – that is now perceived to be the supposedly evil purpose of Islamic 'fundamentalism'. Government is about fostering or preserving the conditions in which capitalist enterprise can create wealth, about a limited equitable distribution, about material welfare, about involvement with specified moral issues involving women's rights, racial parity, cultural pluralism, approved sexual conduct, and so forth – but in each case with no canopy of agreed philosophy beneath which they are to be legitimized. It is simply assumed that each rapid enlargement of the State's involvement in such matters is self-evidently desirable – usually by appeal to material self-interest or to the concept of a pluralism of values.

Whilst paradoxically extremely prescriptive in some areas – race equality, for example – the modern State regards itself as being only the neutral guardian of a pluralism of values and beliefs in some others. Most of these others turn out to be what governments have in the past considered to be their essential purpose, the justification for their existence. They have to do with the embodiment of religious teaching, the service of the gods, the enactment of moral law perceived to have transcendent authority, and similar matters once thought to be fundamental to civilized human association. The modern State regards these to be controversial, and regards itself as no longer possessed of the competence to judge, let alone endorse, one in preference to another. The modern movement of people, caused by economic forces, refugees escaping violence, and the availability of efficient transport, has mixed up peoples and religions and cultures, and all the indications are that this is set to continue. The result, the 'society of plural values', is what liberal governments today, of all the leading political parties, consider it their duty to protect. Once a higher vocation for the State has been in practice abandoned, government itself becomes a matter of regulating consumption, providing material welfare, and, in a very limited manner, so it seems, attending to a just distribution. Politicians still often employ the rhetoric of higher ideals; they apply it, however, to what inevitably turns out to be the lower needs of material welfare. In the education of children, furthermore, the State declines to endorse a specific philosophical or religious interpretation of the world, and the highest ethical ideal peddled in the classroom is 'caring'.

In fact the concept of a society of plural values is not new. Very many societies of the past consisted of a multiplicity of religious cults and practices, of different concepts of moral law or of principles of government. Conditions within the Roman Empire, at the time when the Christian Church spread, showed this in a very clear manner. So did numerous parts of the Mediterranean world both before and after. In those societies, however, it was always expected that a governing group would impose their view of the State, and their religion and culture, and sub-groups would be accorded, in favourable circumstances, a measure of toleration provided that they met certain obligations – the payment of tax being the major one. Thus within the Islamic states, which were set up after the conquest of early Christendom after the seventh century, Christian believers were allowed a reasonable toleration on the condition that they complied with tax requirements. The notion that it is possible for a state to exist which did not, in some sense, embody a single and identifiable purpose, and in correspondence with some transcendent idea, was unheard of. Such a condition could not, by definition, be civilized. The ancient world, and the Christian Church with it, accepted that people are reared in a moral environment, and that the purpose for which children are socialized, therefore, had to correspond to the moral or religious system from which it was derived. The élite who set the terms of reference in this process could well, and usually did, extend toleration to others – especially to conquered peoples – but did not envisage removing the higher calling from the foundations of the State merely because it did not achieve majority assent. The educative influences of the State were often, in a pre-collectivist age, conveyed through religious cults or institutions; the limited powers of the State, as, again, envisaged before the rise of collectivism in the last two centuries, meant that much activity fell outside its jurisdiction. But it was nearly always accepted that the moral basis of the state would only be constructed and sustained where a single theoretical system legitimized it. In some measure humans are creatures of their moral environment, and are what the conditioning of society makes them. There used to be no sense that all systems are of equal validity, and thus a just government is deemed to be one which enables individuals to choose their favoured one. The modern practice of democratic rights exercised within a pluralism of cultural and moral values does not *act* as if this is the case either. What it does in reality is to prescribe and enforce some moral ideas – the 'politically correct' ones of our own day – and to leave others (the traditionally important ones, about religious or philosophical beliefs) to private choice. To put it more bluntly, the modern liberal State enforces material values, such as human claims to equality or to welfare, and leaves values derived from non-materialist philosophies or religious systems to be selected randomly. It is the triumph of materialism.

Does the Christian Church believe that how the nature of government is arranged is of importance in how values are expressed and transmitted? Does it teach, therefore, that the State should recognize, in some sense, the existence of higher ideals – even of divine revealed laws? Or does the Church suppose that others, who do believe the State should embody approved ideas – like the secular materialists – should be allowed to operate the instruments of social control because the present operators say that will tolerate a multiplicity of moral systems? If the State no longer exists to embody and promote higher purposes, but is an affair of management and welfare, does the Church suppose that this is, in itself, an implementation of the love of neighbour enjoined in the Gospel? Is it desirable to move towards an acknowledged *secular* state, on grounds of justice, since it alone might preserve individual rights to private choice of values in a plural society? Secular states are actually very difficult to envisage, since the necessary compulsions required to legitimize order are always in correspondence with sacral values of some sort – even if never precisely or consciously defined: does the Church therefore have a view on any limits which may be set to the moral competence of the State? Because there seems no possibility in existing circumstances for Christians themselves to desire a return to the 'Christendom model', where the Church seeks to use the machinery of worldly govern-ment to embody ideas derived from revelation, does this mean that they are unprepared to identify *any* theoretical system which could legitimize the basis of the State? The world now has a growing number of examples where the old 'Christendom model' is being used to set up governments dedicated to a rule informed by religious teaching: Islamic revivalism. On the face of it, Western Christians seem to regard this development with horror, yet it is simply a return to normality in preceding human affairs, and how the Church itself behaved politically for the best part of two thousand years where it had the chance. Does the modern repulsive rejection of the 'Christendom model' by believers today indicate that *all* attempts to make the State embody Christian moral law *because it is Christian* will find no acceptance? Is the Church to regard itself as only pressing for particular legislative enactments when it supposes them to be incorporated into a moral consensus with other religions and with the secular humanists? Does, therefore, its present tendency to envisage the Church as one only of a number of 'faith communities' render it just one among a number of pressure-groups who may address the State for specific desired ends? What kind of limits does it imagine the dogma of democracy imposes on its preparedness to endorse ideas which are potentially or actually outside the liberal consensus – a consensus which now operates according to precepts derived largely from materialist presuppositions?

On these and similar questions the Church of England is silent. Yet the nature of Political Science, the arrangement of life in society, has through the centuries been a major preoccupation of its scholars and governors, as they have sought to determine the nature of the Christian vocation in the world. Since the Greek Sophists, the noblest minds have addressed issues which touch the basic principles of human association; in their place, today, modern Anglicans go on about immigration law or welfare benefits. And this is represented by them – when they feel the need for justification at all – as a moral advance. For they have had done with all the messy ideological divisiveness of the past, and are now, they suppose, really getting down to 'caring' about human need. For 'human need' read materialism, however, and all their ethical declamations may actually be heard as little more than acceptance of the attitudes of a society absorbed by its own pursuit of welfare and security.

The issues and ideas involved in determining whether the State should embody higher ideals, and whether these ideals should have majority assent among the governed, remain tantalizingly difficult. There is an area of Christian inquiry which needs urgent attention, before the Church of England, and the other Churches in Western societies, are irretrievably absorbed by materialist political ideas. There are two immediate problems – leaving aside the really difficult theoretical ones – and Anglicans are, once again, declining to recognize them. The first is that ideas in Political Science do not derive from consensus: they are inherently controversial. Since the golden rule of modern Church leaders is the avoidance of controversy – which they see as detrimental to their career prospects – there is little chance that they will look with favour on any serious attempt to question the values of existing political debate. The second is that very few of them are intellectually equipped to do so. The educational achievements of the higher clergy, and the clergy of all sorts, come to that, are in sharp decline relative to the accomplishments of professionals in general. It would be instructive to know how many of them have read a word of Plato.

There appears to be very little criticism of modern capitalism in the Church of England. Again, there is a contrast with opinion as it was thirty or forty years ago, when Church bodies, and the clergy in their pulpits, were frequent in their assaults upon capitalist practices and ideas, and when the multi-national corporations, as they were then described, came under particular vilification. Can it now be said that, following the Thatcher revolution in economic attitudes, the Church of England is friendly to capitalism? If so, the change is a remarkable one. Ever since the later years of the nineteenth century the more energetic and idealistic of the clergy had spoken out against the capitalist system – it became an article of faith in 'Christian Socialism', to which many of the leaders of the Church, through bodies like the Christian Social Union, gave their support. Has that all now gone away? It looks a lot like it, though judgement can only be made by negative deduction. There is little positive appraisal of neo-capitalism in the Church, but no criticism either. Through its own investment policies the Church of England is plainly dependent upon the operations of the market (and their stake in it) for a large part of its income: but then it was also at the time when the clergy were dedicated critics of capitalism. The Church of England was never noted for consistency.

Modern capitalism in England – in the last fifteen years, let us say – has produced grotesque contrasts in the distribution of wealth. The Church would seem to have behaved as if this is morally acceptable, or perhaps as if it is something outside its terms of reference. Capitalists always seek to maximize their profits, and when the less well-off begin to achieve purchasing capacity, as at present, it is inevitable that the market will attend to their demands, whatever their quality in cultural terms. The result is a gravitational pull downwards in the cultural values of capitalist society: the 'dumbing down' noticed in public debate. As the Church is so implicated in capitalist practices it might have been expected that it would declare a public view on this matter, too. Once more it is silent. Dependence on the market for so much of its income, and the decline in church attendance, and therefore of a reliable basis for voluntary donations, are producing a financial crisis of august proportions. Even this, however, does not appear to be prompting any scrutiny of capitalist procedures within the Church. As so often in its past, the Church of England is content to accept the values of the society within which it is set – or, to be more precise, the values and practices of its governing elites.

This brings us to the question of 'family values', the centrepiece of such social doctrine as the Church possesses at the present time. Almost nothing so accessibly demonstrates the proximity of modern Anglicanism to the values of bourgeois society as does its endorsement of the bourgeois concept of the family. For the model of family values is not derived from a

wide overview of historical experience, or from a scan
of existing social realities, but from the practices of
middle-class families. The key concept is stability.
The family is not imagined in terms of the extended
families of the past, or of working-class society in
more recent times, in which children were nurtured
in the rough-and-tumble of quite large families, but
as the tight, small units of modern bourgeois practice.
These are the product of social aspiration, the pursuit
of respectability, of contraception and abortion, of a
sense that the 'quality of life' is enhanced if expectations are not blighted by the expense of more than a
couple of children. There is no real evidence that
small family units, and 'stable relationships', provide
the best environment for the rearing and socializing
of children. Best for what, anyway? Does it mean that
such an arrangement is most conducive to the production of people who will sustain the system that
produced them? Married life has many advantages,
and not least that it is, Christians believe, the condition in which human sexuality is most providentially
exercised. But married life does not, of itself, furnish
the stable and serene environment posited in modern
Anglican assessment. It is a device, an arrangement:
it is better not to start confusing it with romantic
love. For most of history, and in many cultures to this
day, marriage was simply an arrangement, fixed up
by social custom. It is modern false expectations of all
marriages harbouring romantic love, together with
personal claims to fulfilment in various ways, which
probably accounts for the enormous divorce rate. The
extent of divorce, as it happens, is actually beginning

to return children to the conditions which were once normal in their upbringing – internal upheaval. In traditional society children were used to having a lowly place in the society of other children in the extended family; they were accustomed to death, with its effect of rapid changes in the family's composition and its destruction of security; and they expected, in a patriarchal order, to be subject to unexplained restraints. The Church of England consecrated such arrangements for centuries. Now it goes on about the 'family values' of modern bourgeois practice. And because it does not wish to deposit itself outside the camp of the politically correct, it has ceased criticizing 'one-parent families' originating outside marriage. What is needed is more clarity about the Church's social policy, just as it is needed in relation to its political teaching. Too much is simply drawn from existing secular practice, with no authentic tradition of Christian thought and learning brought to bear upon it. Prophetic judgement is a crucial dimension of Christian service: not a great deal of it seems to be going on.

4

Ambiguous ethical teaching: 2. Human sexuality

When the American Episcopal Church decided, in the summer of 2003, to proceed with the consecration of an actively homosexual priest as a bishop, it caused an international sensation. The English Church had itself just managed to escape precipitating the same crisis by the use of discreet personal pressure applied outside of the public gaze; the Americans are more open in the conduct of their procedures. The events in both countries, and elsewhere, are proving – not surprisingly – to have far-reaching consequences for the Anglican Communion. In America the debate about the nature of sexuality, and the place of homosexual Christians in the Church, had a certain ideological clarity, for it was expressed frankly in the secular language of rights and social inclusion. Little pretence was made about 're-interpreting' past teachings hostile to homosexual behavior; they were simply jettisoned. The liberals responsible for the new policy, and the new teachings implicit in it, merely accepted what seemed to them to be self-evident – that where the traditional attitudes of the Church were found to be incompatible with modern morality, and the data upon which it is based, they should be changed. The

ferocity with which liberals espouse the new enlightenment of our times is nowhere so evident as in
America, where the agenda of much religious reflec-
tion on everything derives from selected streams of
current secular thinking and practice. It is all about
'issues'. Liberals refer to the past, and point out that
the Church once accepted slavery and the social sub-
servience of women, and that Biblical teachings in
those areas, and others, had been abandoned in the
light of modern moral constructions. Neither of these
two particular issues, as it happens, are helpful as
pointers in the admittedly difficult adjustments
which sometimes have to be made in order to represent Christian truths in the moral understanding of
contemporary society. One problem is that there is
rarely a single moral understanding, but a texture of
disagreements and rival contentions. Another is that
issues like slavery and the position of women only
assume the function of crucial moral tests when the
educated classes have decided they should: the historical record suggests that in preceding practice both
were regarded as matters of social status in a hier-
archical society which did not regard them to be of
significant moral value. Social status, like social
custom, inevitably changes with circumstance and the
passage of time. The individual's use of his own
body, in response to sexual impulsions, however, is
timeless, and the Christian Church has always (until
now) insisted that there are some types of behaviour
which are in all conditions wrong.

In the case of homosexual behaviour – since this is
the matter which prompted the prevailing Anglican

crisis – some revision of attitudes to the matter are plainly needed in the light of modern knowledge about the origins of individual sexual orientation, but essential teaching also needs to be looked at closely to determine exactly what it was that the Church disallowed in the past. And what emerges is that there was never a condemnation of homosexuality as such – no word existed for the condition – but only for the actions associated with it. Love between people of the same sex, which had undoubted erotic undertones but was not expressed physically, was simply an observable phenomenon in the ancient world – throughout the society in which the Early Church formulated its moral teaching. It was not conceivable that God would send people into the world with intense sexual feelings which were in themselves corrupt: love had noble qualities, which, when authentic, were always accepted. This is not to say that whatever is natural is good. Homosexuals are conditioned by influences at an early stage in life, when they have no control over the means by which their sexual orientation is determined. But so are those who become paedophiles or necrophiliacs. An external moral law is then brought to bear in determining what is acceptable and what is not. Hence the need to identify exactly what Christian moral law comprises. What was condemned by the Church were *acts*. Certain sexual acts were considered perversions of the Providential scheme for human continuity, for procreation, and were condemned. Sexual commissions of these sorts were regarded as no part of the Christian life, whether evidenced as expressions of heterosexual or homosexual affection. The human person, furthermore, is easily overtaken by them, so that sexual desire gains an ascendancy: then begins a corrupted life of fornication, of licentiousness, of promiscuous associations. God does not condemn homosexuals or the noble instincts disclosed within homosexual eroticism: what God hates is sexual acts which gratify lust, simulate acts of procreation, use the bodies of others for merely physical sensations of pleasure.

In a materialist society sex tends to be defined *solely* as a series of *acts*, which the person may or may not gratify according to personal inclination or, if appropriate, the compliance or availability of a partner. 'Love' is brought on as a dimension of 'caring', and is considered important but, for many, not a necessary ingredient. There is less sense that human sexuality assists enormously in the definition of the person, and has moral constraints intended to correspond with all the other inhibitions which constitute a well-ordered life. As a consequence there is little inclination to contemplate the existence of attraction between people which, though undoubtedly sexual in nature, is not a suitable reason for a sexual act. Sex has come to be equated with sexual commission. In the real world of human experience, however, very many experiences of sexual attraction have, in the nature of things, to be left unexplored. Whoever sees a woman and lusts after her, as Jesus said, has committed adultery in his heart.

In the realm of sexual action there is a simple Christian law which covers both heterosexual and homosexual love, and adherents of Christianity are asked to respect it. Those who, for whatever reason, are unable to enter into sexual partnerships which associate sexuality with human reproduction, and the creation of the society in which children are to be nurtured, are called to celibacy. That does not mean that homosexuality is a sin. It is, on the contrary, a gift from God, and enrichment of human understanding for those who find themselves to be homosexual; Christians are called to renounce *acts* of the body which are liable to corrupt them. The problem with modern advocates of accepting homosexual *acts* as legitimately Christian is that they accept, as part of that, the homosexual sub-culture of current materialist Western society, with its obsessive gratification and serial relationships. It is no great help, for moral clarity, to declare that 'monogamous' homosexual partnerships must be accorded moral parity with heterosexual ones, since they are extremely rarely arrived at without preceding experiments in promiscuous liaisons, and have no possible procreative intent. Heterosexuals should note this, too: in modern Western society their seemingly increasing liability to practise free sex might well be – as by the Church in the past – condemned in as strong a tone as homosexual promiscuity, as licentiousness. The body is the temple of the soul. It shapes our understanding of ourselves and our purpose, and the beginning of all education in spirituality is self-discipline. Sexual orientation appears to be fixed by early experiences over which the individual has no control: this is also another reason for not considering it, in itself, as corrupt. It is involuntary, a morally neutral condition until given overt expression. What individuals can control is sexual action, and that is very much an area of moral choice, which helps to define what each person is. Christian homosexuals are as much members of the Church as anyone else who accepts the call of Christ, and should receive, as in the past, posts within the ministry if that is deemed to be the will of Christ. Homosexuals have observably been an enrichment of the Church – as the record of the past shows – and the moral beauty of their sense of love has served its purposes. But they are people whose sacrificial giving includes abstention from sexual commissions which the Church has always taught to be, whether practised by heterosexuals or homosexuals, wrong in all circumstances. The sexualization of modern Western popular culture, and the ethical crudity of much public debate of moral 'issues', makes this a difficult distinction to make in these days. People have come to see sexual expression, and the inclusiveness and parity of sexual acts, as *rights*, and hence the language of rights in which the discussion of homosexuality in the Church is now so often conducted. Liberal views about homosexual acts constitute part of political correctness; restrictive opinions about sexuality are regarded as unhealthy.

This analysis is running into greater detail than it needs to; the point is that serious enquiry into the nature of the past teachings and moral attitudes of the Church is neither extensive enough nor informed enough to be of service in existing controversy. There should be more of such enquiry. The leaders of the Church of England, characteristically, sought to overcome short-term problems in the debate about homosexuality by devising forms of words to which the different parties could assent – general expressions so imprecise as to be universally inclusive. They saw their primary duty as the preservation of the unity of the Church. But the Churches which make up the Anglican Communion do not have much unity anyway, and many of them are deeply divided internally. There are differences of interpretation between liberals and traditionalists, Evangelicals and the rump of the High Church, those who believe Christianity to be true and those who suppose it a quasi-mythical starting point for personal enquiry into meaning. When the various constituent Churches of the Anglican Communion abandoned the Book of Common Prayer, in the 1970s, they lost in practice their only real bond of union. It is difficult to see how these Churches can be regarded as 'in communion' when even matters of obviously shared order, like the ordination of women or the acceptance of active homosexuality, are each determined separately by the member churches. Lambeth Conference resolutions and declarations are purely advisory, and few lay people would appear to be advised by them. The Church of England itself exists in a state of internal schism, the more remarkable for being the only example in Church history of a schism set up by the leaders of the Church themselves. This occurred a decade ago, in the provision of parallel episcopal oversight for parishes unable to accept the priesthood of women. The Church of England is in practice two communions, not one; which makes the attempt to preserve 'unity' over the question of homosexuality appear, to put it no more forcefully, rather artificial. The situation for English Anglicans is even more baffling since the General Synod has accepted the legitimacy of homosexual conduct by the laity – introducing only the saving caveat that it is a lifestyle which 'falls short of the Christian ideal' – whilst simultaneously prohibiting the clergy from tasting the forbidden fruit. This is not a love that dare not speak its name but one whose name differs between clergy and laity.

In allowing things to get to this incoherent mess the leadership of the Church has much to answer for. The priority of preserving a union which has only extremely intangible existence, and by the deployment of verbal formulae which are plainly equivocations, is a species of 'statesmanlike' craft easily recognizable as a dimension of British pragmatism, discernable across the face of public life. But as the compromises and carefully devised ambiguities begin to stack up over the years, the result, as may now be seen, is an institution which exists to preserve itself rather than to promote truth. The extraordinary thing about the Church of England is that they all spend so much time attempting to avoid controversy yet are permanently enveloped in it. All their geese, as they say, are swans. Since the pursuit of truth has always been a divisive matter, as reference to the history of the Church will show, it is probably better to fall apart over really important issues in the definition of sound teaching than over preserving a palpable institutional chaos.

Except for those immediately involved, the question of the Church's teaching on homosexuality must seem something of a sideshow. It is the modern Church's failure to address its members on matters involving sexual morality in general which is most liable to cause it damage in the long term. It is not that the Church does not have a moral theology in such areas but that it does not teach the one it has got. The pulpits are silent; few priests advise their flocks about the standards – and sacrifices – required of Christians in sexual behaviour. To some extent, it is true, this is based on ordinary cowardice: they know that the laity expects to arrive at their own opinions on such matters, and that any declarations by them which appear to contradict them will prompt controversy. It is puzzling that they should allow the present situation to continue, all the same. For the laity usually derive their moral opinions from media discussions, and from the manner in which news items touching such issues as medical technology are presented by liberal commentators and supposed experts. Lay knowledge of Christian moral theology, and its historical development, is in general negligible. Decisions and judgements are therefore arrived at by those possessed of only one side of each case. Additionally, the presentation of religious attitudes to human sexuality in schools has been, over the past thirty years or so, either open-ended, in order that the children may determine what are imagined to be their own views, or else a texture of liberal propaganda represented as objectively-based data about human sexuality. The clergy of the day share many of these opinions, and acquire them in the same way; the main reason for their failure to make public declaration of the Church's official teaching on sex, however, is not seeping liberalism, and a consequent disinclination to believe their own Church's moral precepts, but dislike of saying anything which will not be popular. Thus the Church's prohibition of divorce, abortion, sexual relations outside marriage, adultery and all kinds of fornication, which are today considered normal sexual practice by heterosexuals, are left unstated. Many, indeed, suppose that it is the Roman Catholic Church alone which has a systematic teaching in such matters. Only in the question of carnal relationships between persons of the same sex has the Church of England been forced into public debate: here it shot itself in the foot, since the issue was raised to prominence, and unavoidable controversy, by the bishops themselves, both in England and America, when attempting to force forward changes in the Church's policy towards homosexual priests. Even then, as recent events have shown, very few clergy resorted to the pulpits to preach principles based on the Church's moral theology: some organized public discussions in which 'all viewpoints' were aired; most ignored the issue to avoid divisive debate of any sort.

What the Church of England's leadership needs first to do is to promote its own teachings. If the number of liberals within its membership is so large that it is difficult to muster enough support for its 'traditional' (i.e. its actual) teaching then there is a real problem. That could well be the case. For half a century or more liberals' beliefs in relation to the moral laws which govern human sexuality have been indistinguishable from those of the secular humanism widespread within educated opinion generally. Their moral attitudes, that is to say, are secularized. They also reflect the popular culture of moral inclusion; a 'judgemental' attitude to sexual morality is to be shunned, and the test of acceptable sexual behaviour identified as 'caring'. In its breezily 'healthy' attitude to sex this inclination to suppose that everything is acceptable provided nobody gets hurt − itself, in all truth, a rare thing to accomplish, anyway − constitutes dozens of moral tableaux in a week of viewing television dramas. In the 1960s the predecessors of modern liberal morality were the progressive theologians with their doctrine of 'situational ethics', in which restrictive rules were to be abandoned because authentic love was imagined to produce, of itself, its own canons of behaviour. A good deal of sophistication went into the articulation of this patent sophistry, and a whole generation of excited seminarists were raised on its heady suppositions. Then came the start of the Evangelical ascendancy in the Church of England, notable by the 1980s, and a rather ineffective brake was applied − ineffective because the liberals remained in their positions of influence, especially in education, and continued their pursuit of humanistic morality. The Evangelicals, in office, began to learn some of the arts of Anglican polity, as well. Their inclination to conservative teaching in sexual morality abruptly ran into the moral illiteracy of the laity, by now well versed in opinions picked up from the media, and the result, as usual, was fear of declaring the Church's own teaching on human sexuality from the pulpit. Nobody wanted to seem old-fashioned, or out of touch with scientific advance. For it is the speed of medical technology, as much as the triumph of liberal humanism, which has changed attitudes – all those television images of cells and embryos being manipulated in order to help childless couples, and so forth; the informed experts, in their surgical get-ups, offering quite unwarranted assurances of the utopia to come. Current humanist sexual morality appears to be planted in hedonism and self-interest: ethical conduct is whatever conduces to welfare. This simple belief is reproduced inside the Church and is imagined to be an application of the Gospel of Christ. Few dare to see it for what it is – the sacralizing of ordinary materialism. For it posits no external laws for human conduct, no commandments made explicit by God on the mountain or in the Church, and no measure for the purpose of human life beyond the pursuit of pleasure.

The one area in which the clergy are explicit and articulate about sexual morality is where it touches 'family values'. Thus adultery continues to be condemned, not so much because it goes against the Ten Commandments but because it is a significant cause of family break-up. Looked at closely, in fact, the Church's endorsement of family values turns out to rest on pragmatic contentions rather than on principles derived from moral theology. Bishops do not say that teachings on the family are inspired by the example of the Holy Family of Nazareth; instead they suggest that they came from the need to sustain a stable environment in which children can be reared. To the extent that family values have an ancient pedigree, indeed, it is not because of any regard for the welfare of children but because of patriarchy – the authority of the senior male over the family clan. It is a point, not surprisingly, overlooked in the modern Anglican appraisal of the virtues of the family as an institution. Nor are 'family values' derived from within the family unit at all: they comprise whatever social or moral values achieve ascendancy in the surrounding culture – the family structure itself merely transmits them to new generations. Since a third of marriages end in divorce, and it is reasonable to suppose that a large number, perhaps equally as large, avoid dissolution but are deeply unsatisfactory as working partnerships, the family can scarcely be considered all that stable as a nurturing environment for children. It also hints at the existence of widespread adultery. The Church is silent on the sexual morality to be followed *inside* marriage; no guidance is given on the various practices, which used to be considered deviant, that now often accompany conventional marital acts and are presented, in popular entertainment, as 'spicing up' a relationship.

What does the Church of England teach about the moral purpose of sexual relations inside marriage? For all the time now given over to the questions relating to homosexuality, it is, in terms of sheer volume, sexual commission between couples who are married which should receive more public explanation. God has providentially linked sexuality and the perpetuation of the species; in sensate beings there is necessarily a moral network of interpretation and law. Christianity has, through the centuries, upheld certain teachings, all of which rested unambiguously on the causal association between sex and the creation of individual lives. Sexual feeling is a bodily appetite, an incentive to action which generates life. In this it is little different from other bodily sensations which induce action necessary for survival: food is pleasurable to eat, but eaten for pleasure alone becomes the occasion of gluttony. Over-indulgence in food prompts ill-health; over-indulgence in sex results in spiritual ill-health – the person becomes absorbed by compulsive sexual feeling and is obsessive in seeking gratification. Traditional Christian teaching rejected acts which destroyed the unwanted consequences of sexual relations: infanticide, abortion, or artificial means of frustrating conception – all widely practised in the ancient world. Their error, or sin, lay not only in their denial of God's providential intention in human sexuality but in elevating personal bodily pleasure. Where the possibility of procreation was eliminated, as in artificial means of birth control, pleasure tends in practice to become the only ground of sexual relations. Some modern Anglican moralists have argued, however, that where this pleasure is mutual it becomes a quasi-sacramental bond of affection between married people, and so, as a 'secondary' purpose, may receive moral approval. In 1930 the Lambeth Conference advised that there were circumstances in which it could be morally acceptable to 'avoid parenthood' in martial relations, and in 1958 the Conference commended 'responsible parenthood'.

Debate on these occasions was much hedged about with consideration of possible medical conditions, or the size of existing families. After 1958, however, there was a rapid advance to the separation of sexual relations inside marriage from moral constraints of any sort, and in the era of AIDS, from the 1980s, churchmen were recommending contraception for those engaged in promiscuous sexual encounters with no pretense of reference to married life at all. For a couple of years after the 1958 Lambeth Conference the largest manufacturer of contraceptives in England included the Lambeth resolutions in each packet – perhaps the last occasion in English history on which the Church will receive the endorsement of the popular culture. In the years which have followed the Church of England's *volte face* on the question of birth-control there has been virtually no internal discussion. Occasionally the Roman Catholic Church has been criticized for its continued adhesion to teaching which has been declared for two thousand years. The results have been enormous. Pleasure has replaced childbirth as the primary purpose of sexual relations inside marriage. Sexual acts have been alienated from a higher purpose, and have become frequent and casual. Sexual incompatibility has risen in public consciousness as justification for ending relationships. Human associations which once found their dignity in the providential scheme are now pursued for selfish ends. What is perceived as gain include enhanced quality of life for both parents and children, some control of the transmission of sexually transmitted diseases, the limitation of population, and pleasure.

Important gains; also important losses. The gains are judged by materialist tests, and the losses by spiritual ones. Bodies have become utilities, at the disposal of their occupants without reference to external moral law. And the Church appears satisfied with the result: artificial contraception is no longer a matter of controversy, at least within Anglicanism. The matter is so completely settled, in fact, that it seems unlikely that Anglican moralists will ever visit it again. No teaching is given about 'responsible parenthood' in the Church – not even, in general, in the preparation of couples seeking Church marriage: it is simply assumed that the morality of contraception is self-evident. The condemnations made by Anglican authorities until the middle years of the last century are entirely forgotten. It cannot even be said that the modern clergy teach the morality, as they see it, of artificial means of birth control; the issue is just not raised; there is no teaching of any sort. But once the link between sex and procreation has been broken it is difficult to see why the Church of England should persist in the belief that sex should only take place inside marriage. This opens up a whole chatroom of moral inconsistencies.

In view of the Church's endorsement of 'family values', it is surprising that it is not more censorious about 'partnerships'. These are practical arrangements in which a couple enter a residential sexual liaison without marriage – until recently called 'living in sin' – which have acquired wide public acceptance in an astonishingly short space of time. Presumably this indicates, once more, the formative influence of television. It is in fact not really surprising that the Church of England does not offer public condemnation of partnerships, as guidance for its own members, because they have become accepted as an article of faith in political correctness. Like one-parent families, and homosexual liaisons, those involved are beneficiaries of social inclusion: judgemental attitudes are no longer considered appropriate. Positive affirmation and approval, in fact, indicate the desire of modern society to distance itself from traditional Christianity. Where religion is valued it is as an affair of indiscriminate benevolence, a consecration of liberal opinions about love without rules – love, in this understanding, excluding some practices, like paedophilia or bestiality, which liberals continue to regard, on rather imprecisely expressed moral principles, as improper. Once a universally accepted moral code (such as traditional Christianity formerly supplied) has been abandoned, as incompatible with the existence of a plural society, there is inevitably a problem about identifying the philosophical system of which current moral practice is an ethical application. In the cases of sex with minors or with animals it is possible to fall back on precepts about free-agency. In the case of sexual partnerships no justification is attempted. To the participants and their politically correct supporters there seems no problem; love provides its own justification. In civilized societies of the past, even in the most pagan of the pagan ancient world, however, sexual liaison was always regarded as a matter of public concern: hence the formalities of marriage, and the part played by the state in their legal observance. 'Partnerships' in modern Western societies are now extremely common, and some of them involve the additional complication of adultery by one or both of the partners.

Many of those presenting themselves to the clergy for a church wedding are at the time living in partnerships, and as this now involves no social stigma, and is only discriminated against at peril to the discriminator, they can see no practical incompatibility between the Church's teaching and their condition. Nor, amazingly, can the clergy, who often seem perfectly willing to proceed with the Church's blessing in full consciousness that the Church's own teachings are being violated in the process. This situation had been prepared by attitudes to divorce. The Church of England very clearly prohibits divorce for its own members, yet there have been bishops in recent times who are themselves divorced. This ought to have prompted the same kind of uproar in the Church as the attempt to consecrate active homosexuals to the episcopate. But it did not. The re-marriage of divorced people by the Church was, until 2002, not allowed under canon law. In that year a permissive system was authorized by Synod in which, at individual clerical discretion, divorced people may receive a Church wedding should they attempt a second essay in the marital state. This extraordinary outcome, to a debate in the Church which had lasted for decades, was justified on what were thought of as 'pastoral' grounds. It actually amounts to the ancient contention always used to rationalize breaking moral law by those who imagine their experience of human love to transcend it, that individual needs are not met by blanket prohibitions. The result, in the case of the re-marriage of the divorced, is that the Church has sanc-tioned the violation of its own teaching in a formal and constitutional manner. Those opposed to this plainly absurd proceeding were made to feel old-fashioned and uncaring. It is always the way. Both in the practical acceptance of partnerships, therefore, and in beginning to dismantle the Church's marriage discipline, the Church of England has confronted the materialism of the modern world and compromised itself. How betrayed all those must feel who, after years of unhappiness in marriages that turned out to be unsuitable, nevertheless stuck to the solemn obligation they undertook before God to remain with their partner 'for better or for worse'. In the age of convenience living there are now disposable ecclesias-tical laws. Similarly over the practice of abortion – the modern resurgence, on a huge scale, of the ancient pagan practice of infanticide – the Church remains silent, leaving it to the Roman Catholics to attract the displeasure of enlightened current opinion. The Church of England has not changed its prohibition of abortion: it simply ignores the whole matter, as if it were not the gravest moral issue of the age. For the laity the matter is regarded as one of individual choice. Most abortions these days are not sought for medical reasons, but because unwanted children are perceived to interfere with the quality of life.

The Church's prophetic office might also have been brought to bear on another current moral phenome-non: the sexualization of the popular culture. Can it really be desirable that it should offer no advice or warning to its members about the representation of social existence as a widening series of occasions for sexual encounter? Again, it is fear of seeming out of touch with the times, or with being personally ill-adjusted to the *mores* of the age, or with having unhealthy inhibitions, that probably explains why the bishops and clergy do not resolutely condemn a culture which is becoming soaked in sexual reference – in almost every double entendre in every television panel game, in every steamy drama, in so many advertisements. Thus human life is represented in its most material form: the appeal of sex without any higher purpose than personal pleasure. But how frightened the clergy are of seeming puritanical; see also how many of them have by now absorbed so much of the popular culture of sexuality that they are no longer conscious of its pervasive influence in their own view of things. It is also safer to join the clamours of the informed for disabled access or racial equality, for then they are in the familiar world of consensus: this will not involve them in controversy. But the Bible is full of exhortations for God's faithful people to eschew corrupt cultures, established in wrong behaviour, and to seek that personal order and self-discipline which is the essential preliminary of spiritual formation. Human sexual action, for Christians, is intended to be sparingly engaged, its significance enhanced by its special quality. Personal restraint, and the high esteem in which physical relations are held, should be, for Christians, a characteristic, an indication that they are separated from the pagan world. They know that sex has compulsive effects if engaged casually, or, as so frequently in the modern world, for entertainment. For today sexual relations have become a leisure activity, and, for those who have become addicted, an obsessive pursuit of pleasure for no more significant reason than that personal desires are gratified. The Church once warned its members about the consequences of sex when practised in separation from serious purpose. And that purpose was represented in procreative intention. When the Church of England added pleasure as a secondary purpose for sexual inter-course, and knowingly encouraged contraception in the process, it assisted a revolution in the commission and understanding of human sexuality. It is leading – as the Roman Catholics had realized – to the unravel-ling of the Church's moral theology on sexuality. The use of the contraceptive pill and of artificial means of birth control should revert to being matters of the most serious moral debate. In primitive societies, where infant mortality was high, and moral law unde-veloped, frequent sexual intercourse helped to replen-ish the earth and provide for the continuation of the species; life was short, humans were more brutish. Christian moral law, however, was formulated for a people with moral choice, with a sophisticated culture, whose human relations were established within frameworks long tested by collective experi-ence – societies in which sexual excesses were con-demned because they were a betrayal of the higher instincts and purposes of life. What higher purposes are served in modern society, whose people routinely expect sexual release to be frequent and casual, whether inside marriage or outside it? The Church should feel an obligation to explain its teachings on sexual morality to its members. It does have such teaching, even if in a compromised form. What it does not do is to make any serious attempt at systematic public declaration – and that just at a time of general moral incoherence, when clarity of statement and sure guidance is needed. The issues involved, it is true, are difficult; the public seems unprepared to listen to any exhortation which encourages restraint. But the Church is intended to announce truth, and it should never expect that to be popular. In committees and synods, in the writings of its preferred sages, in the muted pulpits of the land, what the public hears from the Church – when it hears anything at all – are the commonplace resonances of the politically correct. Its teaching on sexual morality, rather like that in the classrooms of the land, is preoccupied with 'family values' (whatever they are) and 'caring relationships'. Centuries of learned writing on moral theology lie unexamined.

5

Establishment

There have been quite a few within the Church of England, especially since the High Church revival of the second half of the nineteenth century, who have questioned the constitutional relationship of Church and State. Throughout most of the nineteenth century English Protestant Dissent consolidated around a call for 'Voluntaryism' in religion, in a notably political series of campaigns which intended, through the sponsorship of *ad hoc* reforms, a formal separation of Church and State. Roman Catholics, except in Ireland, were reluctant to join this movement of opinion: the Vatican upheld, as a general principle, that the proper operations of government required the consecration of religion – even if it was Protestant, as in England – and traditional 'Old Catholic' families, anyway, were often closely integrated with the settled structure of local social custom which assumed the continued existence of the State Church. With the High Church revival within the national Church itself, however, an increasing critique of erastian practices began to acquire philosophical overtones: the continuation of the Church as a constitutional Establishment began to appear as a hindrance to spiritual autonomy, which it certainly was, and as an external sign that the Church of England was too intimately associated with prevailing social authority. This second point was also true; it corresponded with the spread of a fashionable 'Christian Socialist' set of postures within the Anglican leadership. The height of internal scepticism about the propriety of a State Church reached its peak in the 1920s, and then began to fall away. The Protestant Dissenters had by then won many of their single-issue reforms, and the main occasion of conflict with the State Church, which was government financial support of Church schools, had ended in a characteristically Anglican compromise – one which was, however, decidedly favourable to the Church of England.

So matters have remained to this day. There has continued to be a small number of Anglican leaders whose opposition to the principle of Establishment is periodically articulated, but the issue, as an issue, has largely been marginalized. With the pressure from Dissent removed – the Free Churches themselves suffering a very significant decline in the twentieth century – and with no political group indicating preparedness to take the matter up, things have quietly passed out of the public mind. Any revival in our day is likely to be defined in reference to the existence of a society of plural values – expressed in ethnic and cultural terms, rather over matters of political theory. In practice, Anglicans critical of Establishmentarianism tend to lose their enthusiasm for change on preferment. The bishops quite like their presence in the House of Lords, and at all levels in the Church there is an illusory sense that the surviving formal trappings of Establishment – attendance at civic dinners, the provision of chaplains for institutions of state and so forth – signify some kind of genuine link to public life.

Any historical survey will show that ideas and practice in the relationship of Church and State in Britain showed some local variations from the European norm, and some local idiosyncrasies, but developments were in correspondence with the experiences of Christendom in general. Constitutional 'Establishments' of Christianity recognized that religion provided the moral foundations; both before and after the events of the Protestant Reformation of the sixteenth century there was a consensus that human association required the consecration of religion for political sanction and the rule of law to achieve an elevation of society above mere order and security. The State was conceived organically: it was possessed of a 'conscience' capable of determining religious truth and deciding which available version should be recognized in the basis of national life. By the first half of the nineteenth century, however, another view had emerged. Distinctively Whig, and anticipating an interpretation of society which conceived itself in atomistic categories – deriving its increasing detachment from the quasi-mystical images of organic concepts of the state from seventeenth-century developments in contract theories of government – this newer understanding regarded the legitimacy of constitutional Establishments of religion as resting upon a majority principle. The Church, for it to have a proper relationship to the State, needed popular support – though by 'popular', in the usage of the times, was actually meant the confidence of the ruling classes rather than the assent of the general population. The genie was out of the bottle. As soon as Christianity effectively ceased to be accorded the protection of the law (and to be recognized as the moral basis of the state and promoted accordingly) solely on the principle of its inherent truth, the first intimations of what, in our own day, was to become the 'plural society', made their appearance. This initially took the form of debate about 'religious toleration'. The logic took a long time to work through, and subsequent changes in the nature both of the State and of society were slow in being recognized. English public life has been conservative as well as pragmatic in point of political development. But the democratization of the Constitution, over half a century, and the erosion of social deference, produced an *ad hoc* demolition of the old Tory political edifice and its ideological justifications: it became obsolete to consider the State to be endowed with a religious conscience, and to consider the Church as the educative and spiritual agent of public will. This large change, and its ancillary consequences, had little to do with the decline of belief in Christianity within the intelligentsia and its clients – although this has became a widely accepted explanation. It had, on the contrary, to do with political and constitutional adjustments made in recognition of diversity *inside* the Christian Churches themselves. The nine-

teenth-century liberal reformers did not seek to usher
in the practical operations of a secular State; they
sought only justice and equality between the various
Christian denominations, an end to the legal pre-emi-
nences of the Established Church. But they opened a
Pandora's box. Soon the pressure was on for constitutional separations of Church and State in Ireland and
then in Wales, and in Colonial and Dominion territo-
ries overseas, for the admission of non-Christians to
political society and to offices of State, and – a development of the later decades of the twentieth century –
for the recognition of the notion that the State existed
to protect a society conceived in frankly pluralistic
terms. In today's political rhetoric this is now
described as 'social inclusion'; its constitutional logic
is a separation of the proceedings of the State from
religious belief altogether. The Victorians had experi-
mented with a kind of halfway house to that destina-
tion, which they called 'concurrent endowment': each
Christian Church was to receive the patronage of the
State and each supported equally. Essays in this practical equality were attempted in relation to Ireland
and the colonies, and in England and Scotland over
parliamentary grants in aid of Christian educational
institutions. The notion has been revived in our own
day in relation to the reform of the House of Lords –
that, instead of removing the Anglican bishops, who
are a remnant of Establishment and organic ideology,
they should be augmented with senior representatives of the other Christian Churches and of other
religious bodies. There are practical problems in this
solution, however, and it is unquestionably defective

in logic: if the State is to recognize religious belief in this fashion, even to the extent of incorporating it into the legislative process, why should it not recognize secular belief systems, or associations of any sort? And who is to determine which are worthy of inclusion? The practical consequence would be the assemblage of something like the Corporate State – whose most recent representations, in Fascist Italy and in Spain, were not without notable drawbacks.

At first viewing it might seem that the British State, following the death of organic theories of the Constitution, is, despite the anomalous surviving religious Establishments in Scotland and England, devoid of ideological reference. Much is made, indeed, of the pragmatism of political ideas. Government seems to be an affair of management, and political parties to measure their degrees of difference in relation to policy variations over welfare issues. Parliamentary life does certainly express a practical secularity; legislation is no longer promoted on the basis that its moral pedigree is an interpretation of Christian truth. It is secular, but it is not empty of ideology, however. Nor does the volume of political explanation issuing from public figures suggest a moral vacuum. In reality the modern State is as confessional as its predecessors – it is just that the secular and materialist humanism which it actually promotes does not have a coherent or recognized label by which it can be identified, even by its own practitioners. As employed in practice the moralism of the day is usually spoken of as 'political correctness', and its conveyance in the media or in the classroom is expressed in terms of the sovereign virtue of 'caring'. Yet no one relates the moral basis to a philosophical framework. It is simply assumed as self-evidently authentic. Although the understanding of humanism is secular and materialistic – in that it is without reference to transcendent ideals or religious moral authority – the leaders of Christian opinion would appear to be among its most enthusiastic advocates, casually assuming that in its moral prescriptions may be identified the central ethical teachings of Christ. For all the declamations about choice and pluralism made in relation to modern liberal political practice the truth is that the core beliefs of this secular humanism are enforced by law in a tightly prescriptive manner, and with an almost puritanical insistence that dissent indicates personal delinquency. The modern State no longer feels that its conscience can sponsor the doctrines of institutional Christianity, but no one is left in any doubt about the sacral nature of the moral structure it *does* uphold. Increasing regulation by the State and its agencies of areas of personal and social conduct, which once were considered matters of basic individual liberty, and beyond its competence, is ushering in a political order which is unquestionably confessional. It is now a criminal offence to speak or to behave in a manner which is at variance with the opinion of the State in such areas as race, gender, welfare and certain expressions of sexuality. Victorian laws, commonly ridiculed for their puritanism and for their support of what were thought to be Christian values, were never extended with such intimacy into private belief and practice. There may be all kinds of defensible reasons why modern people allow themselves to be regulated by the State to this extent; the consequence, however, is not a truly liberal polity but one which represents a very high level of prescribed and compulsory moral action.

The modern State is a confessional state: it has simply chosen to replace identifiably Christian teaching with the incoherently rendered tenets of humanism. A simple example: experiments with genetical engineering which once (had such engineering been known about) would, in a Christian state, have been justified according to a formulation of moral understanding supposedly and intentionally derived from Christian teaching, are now accorded a moral basis drawn up by state-appointed 'ethical' consultative committees who appear to determine their much-vaunted moral priorities by whatever is perceived to be of material benefit to humans. They do not adduce their recommendations from a recognizable body of philosophical doctrine. The effective separation of Church and State, therefore, may be seen to have resulted, not in attempts to define an alternative justification for coercive legislation, but the gradual, piecemeal, and philosophically undefined assemblage of a new confessionalism. Church and State have not really been separated at all, in reality – it is simply that 'Church' can no longer be taken to mean the plainly ailing C. of E., but a randomly accumulated mass of regulatory agencies whose only common characteristic is that they are obviously secular and equally obviously unable to explain the moral pedigree of their authority. Thus this is not an age which seeks 'the separation of Church and State'. What it contemplates is the replacement of a constitutional anomaly, the Established Church of England, by a moral anonymity – but a secular 'Church' nonetheless. Any discussion of the question of disestablishment in England should recognize that it is, in effect, not about the removal of the compelled moral teaching of a Church, but a decision about which 'Church' should receive constitutional pre-eminence – the secular 'Church' of materialist humanism or the surviving remnants of institutional Christianity. There is no possibility of formulating a basis for the State which has no moral statements at all, nor is that either possible or desirable: law requires the sanction of morality. And anyway the compulsive moralism of those engaged in the political processes would not allow it.

How did this condition of things come to pass? Opponents of the continuation of formal links of Church and State generally contend that it is merely the recognition of social and cultural pluralism. English society, they argue, no longer has a unitary basis, but should be seen as a pattern of diversities; there is no longer a majority culture which can be taken as a kind of benchmark of national cultural identity, but, in its place, a landscape of minorities, each one of whose cultural and (if they have them) religious values should be recognized as of equal value. The political art is one of 'celebrating diversity' and incorporating all the dimensions into the life of the State. This view of things – which finds its emphasis on cultural relatively echoed in the growing enthusiasm for multi-faith worship and for impre-cisely defined religious ideology – is made to depend on ethnic diversity. In reality the cultural and moral pluralism long ante-dates the immigrations of the mid-twentieth century, and may also be traced to the failure of the State-sponsored Church successfully to accommodate the Christian understanding of large numbers of people. It was the rise of religious dissent which laid the foundations of pluralism in England, and it was the Nonconformists' aspirations for reli-gious equality, and the opening up of the political Constitution to those who were not members of the Established Church, which ushered in liberal concepts of limiting the capacity of the State to pre-scribe and to intervene in the ultimate matter of reli-gious belief. The growth of non-religious critiques of the political processes, the decline of religious belief within the intelligentsia, and the arrival of (relatively small) numbers of immigrant people from non-Christian parts of the world, were minor contributory causes of the accumulating perception that institu-tionalized Christianity could no longer be regarded as an appropriate means of defining the moral identity of the State. The simple view that modern pluralism is in large measure a consequence of ethnic mixture also ignores the extent to which the traditional adhesion of the Constitution to the Church of England represented social class preferences by former political and landed elites. The supposed unitary society of the past, and its political superstructure, never existed in the manner imagined: what existed, on the contrary, was a conflict of classes, with the State Church as among its major beneficiaries – the social proximity of parsons and squires, the clerical magistrates, the erastian system of patronage, the legislative functions of the episcopate and the Supreme Governorship of the Church by the Crown, being among its external manifestations.

Even had there once been, in the span of modern historical development, a significant cultural uniformity, it would not have been a justification for the Establishment of the Church. For that justification lay in the truth of the doctrines taught by the Church, not in mere numbers. In the present 'Establishment' of humanist ethics the same principle operates. The various dogmas of 'political correctness' are enshrined in law not because they are widely believed: on the contrary, many are unpopular – though the effective moral propaganda which promotes them through the legislative programme, through the indoctrination of children in the schools, and through the elites who determine what is disseminated in the media, will in due time change that. At present many are still not a reflexion of the popular will, but the imposition of the values of liberal agencies and pressures. The issue is confused and difficult to analyse: some advances of state control, like the punishment of sex offenders, are welcomed by the public, and are, indeed, promoted by governments for populist reasons; some, on the other hand, are seen by the public as an unwarranted intrusion by the State – the compulsion to employ minorities in order to promote ethnic equality, for example. Public figures themselves, in the vanguard of political correctness, may well determine their endorsement of the new canons by a species of self-interest: they are terrified of the consequences should they fall into the abyss of failing to conform to the new enlightenment. It was ever so. English public life at the present time is not in a stable moral condition; it is in transition from the orthodoxies of the past, which were rendered in the available values and institutions of the Church, to an unknown future, whose foundations, being put down now, would appear to be fashioned out of secular and humanist materials. So far these last are being rather randomly assembled; the building to be reared upon the enthusiasm for human values which inspires the secular polity still to come has no visible shape.

What the secular prophets of the present time assume, however, is that it is possible to defy the experiences of past ages, and the spectacularly dismal human record, and to create a truly tolerant society governed by a political order which recognizes moral and cultural diversity and renounces the relevance of theoretical apparatus altogether. Some even refer to the 'death of ideology' in the modern British State. They are mistaken, wrongly supposing that their inability to attach a philosophical label to the secular humanism they are in fact incorporating into the moral basis of the State renders it somehow value-free, a kind of self-evident and practical tissue of decencies. Nothing in the ingredients of the modern world indicates the demise of ideological conflict, however, and the wise observer will not mistake

sequences of transition, or the obscuring rubble of col-
lapsed traditional structures, for permanent conditions. The moral basis of the British State is at
present there for the taking.

The Established Church, the Church of England,
has lost the will to define its vocation in public life in
terms which correspond to its traditional functions.
That is understandable enough, in view of the decline
of public support for institutional religion and the
growing secularity of the State. But the thinking of
Church leaders would seem to extend considerably
further than a simple abandonment of the past. They
tend now to espouse with enthusiasm the very
concepts of welfare humanism, of moral and cultural
pluralism, and even, in growing numbers, the fostering of religious relativity (multi-faith initiatives in its
educational and worshipping enterprises), which are
the indicators of their own replacement. Instead of
regarding the question of the relationship of Church
and State, of the moral basis of law, as one of the
great themes in Political Science – as a matter which
has occupied the minds of the greatest scholars since
the Greek Sophists – modern Church leaders seem
content to discuss disestablishment, when they
discuss it at all, in pragmatic terms. For very many,
the determining consideration is not the vocation of
the State, but the attempt to define a function for the
Church in a society which is disclosing an indifference
to its existence. They accept, that is to say, the prevalent values of political society, and identify themselves as one of the components of the social
pluralism, possessed of no greater significance than

the others beyond a vague sense that they represent an aspect of national heritage. Their ethicism, including the very content of their moral opinions, is indistinguishable from the chatter of the chattering classes.

It is a remarkable feature of the emergent secular clerisy, of people in public life, that they are highly selective in their overview of society. While much is made of the acceptance of capitalism in the last twenty years, of the withdrawal of the State from direct conduct of economic enterprises, and of a liberalizing of the laws in a few areas (of human sexuality, divorce, artistic censorship, and so forth) the fact is that the power of the State has continued to extend itself in almost every other area. The State may no longer run things, but it *regulates* them instead. This network of regulation, in reality, is state control by sleight of hand, and it is ushering in a massive diminution of individual liberty. The fear of crime, the obsession with health and safety, the public demand that someone should be held accountable for the ordinary misfortunes of life, a vast list of claims for protection against accidents in the operation of public utilities, the persistent call for the confinement of sexual deviants, and so forth, is creating a monolithic structure of State intervention. That the powers this involves are often exercised by separate regulatory agencies, or by local government, does not diminish the nature of the powers themselves. And all this is usually popular, even though there are complaints about some of the accompanying bureaucracy. People now expect to be regulated; they regard it as a dimension of welfare and safety. They may complain, also, when dislocations occur in the accumulating system, or they may disagree with individual cases of regulatory authority, but all indications suggest that people are willing accomplices in public control. The age of individual liberty – that great legacy of the Victorian bourgeoisie – seems set in decline. How is all this pertinent to a discussion of Church and State relations? The answer is simple: the new secular 'Church', as the humanist inspiration of all this gathering collectivism, is the only available successor to the poor old Church of England as the moral basis of national association. The disestablishment of the Church would only recognize, frankly and lucidly, what has already happened in practice – that the will to endorse institutionalized Christianity has largely passed away and that in its place there is a working constitution which is secular, collectivist, and achieves public acceptance. It is now widely accepted as the provider of ethical structures – of all the processes of regulation. The State itself has become the Church.

There cannot be a moral vacuum at the centre of the life of the state; citizens may reasonably ask why they should obey the law, and what it is, philosophically considered, that legitimizes the actions of those charged with government. Since all law ultimately rests upon ethical sanctions, the pedigree of the moral code whose application results in the legislative process ought to be evident to the governed. At the present time, in England, it is not – except to the extent that the anomalous survival of the Church of

England as the Established or State Church, in at least constitutional formality, seems to furnish the ethical foundations. The reality, as suggested already, is that government has become an unidentified version of materialist humanism, to which those in public life actually appeal in justification of law. Instead of regarding the present failure to define the moral basis of the State as a characteristic of the larger transition, from the disintegration of the ancient organic state to the materialist collectivism which is fast accumulating, observers and participants of public life consider it reasonably stable. Politicians, like bishops, are not greatly given to forward planning; they do not look beyond their own retirement or, as in the case of the politicians, beyond the clamour of their constituents for material benefits at the next election. Before long, none the less, versions of the ideological conflict always raging in other theatres of the global human drama will catch up with them. The most immediate complication in any analysis of Church and State relations in England, however, must arise from the increasing incompetence of the existing Established Church to fulfil its duties as a State Church.

With very few remaining who persist in supposing that, even if the State has the capacity to recognize religious truth it would recognize the Church of England rather than, let us say, a broader recognition of several faiths, there is little public will to maintain the existing settlement. The Establishment probably still satisfies a latent sense, in the wider society, that Christianity – defined so imprecisely, as is the

English way, as to amount to little more than a dis-
position to decent behaviour – is part of national
identity. But within the thinking of the governing
elites there is very little of such sentiment left. They
notice that public residual feeling supports, for
example, capital punishment for sexual crimes and
murder, or attitudes to immigration which disguise
pretty unreconstructed racism. Like the old advocates
of the Establishment of the Church on the basis of the
truth of the doctrines it teaches, rather than on the
majority principle applied to the extent of its public
support, the liberal guardians of modern secular government (the educators, the media, and even most
leaders of the Church of England) believe that the
existence of a plural society does not inhibit their
duty to enforce uniform *secular* concepts of public
policy. Since they often do this by actually appealing
to the realities of cultural and moral diversity, as
evidence that ancient support for the Church is
merely the agenda of a minority, the matter is
extremely confused. Yet it does not seem so. British
constitutional theory used to assume that government led opinion, and did not follow it; members of
parliament were representatives of the people and
not delegates. Modern politicians still behave as if
that is the case, though few demonstrate frankness
on the matter. Whatever meaning can be teased
out of the general pragmatism, none the less, and
however incoherent modern attitudes to the practice
of democracy are, especially in a class society like
England, the notion that the Church of England is
any longer a suitable basis for maintaining the

moral fabric of the State appears increasingly arcane.

Inside the Church itself the same range of divided opinion is to be encountered over the great ethical issues of the day as is to be found in secular society. Church leaders defend their constitutional privilege as the Established Church largely on pragmatic grounds, anyway, and few of the bishops in the House of Lords debate ethical questions from the authority of Christian doctrine: their arguments are usually derived from the pervasive secular discourse about social welfare. The growing consideration of the relationship of Church and State itself, in fact, is indicating another feature of the Church of England today: its collapse into itself, its sectarian self-identity, its preoccupation with its internal organization and peculiar customs. Leaders of the Church generally discuss the future of the Establishment in relation to the welfare of the Church itself, what tends to its preservation at a time when, to many external observers, it would appear to be approaching its terminal sequences. But the really important issues in the debate should be about the effect of disestablishment on the *State;* this great issue of Church and State relations has concerned political scientists for over two thousand years, and a huge literature on the subject now lies unexamined on library shelves while the bishops and the politicians exhaust their rhetoric on merely pragmatic and almost wholly transient matters. If the Church of England really is a part of the universal Church, as it claims to be, then whether it is in a formal relationship to the state ought to be, to it, a question of relative indifference. Establishment is a service the Church performs, set up upon terms which have long ceased to recognize political and social realities. If a constitutional severance of the link with government should result in the whole thing falling apart then it will be recognized as never having been a real Church anyway – but a parliamentary fix, cobbled together in the sixteenth century, never defined satisfactorily, in order to achieve, as was supposed at the time, dynastic stability for the House of Tudor.

A separation of the constitutional links of Church and State would obviously affect the role of the Crown. But the removal of the Supreme Governorship of the Church would only return the monarchy to the position it was in before the Reformation. There is no sense in which its constitutional legitimacy would be diminished, or the case for its own abolition advanced. A measure of constitutional tidying up – in relation to the succession, and so forth – would be necessary. The ideological consequences of a separation would be felt in the Church: the withdrawal of the Royal Supremacy would, in theory, leave the Church of England without a means of determining its own basis of authority, since it has no access to General Councils of the universal Church, and a devolved synodical structure of governance which excludes doctrinal definition from its competence. There is no Royal Supremacy over the Church in the Scottish (Presbyterian) Establishment, and that is not regarded, in itself, as compromising the existence of monarchy.

To some the Church of England will today appear simply no longer qualified to be the confessor of the State, and for no more complicated reason than that the State is in practice already secular. They may well ruminate upon the former political utility of the Church, stir up its ethical embers, and see if there is much life left in it. They may not see much. The Church of England, like institutional religion generally in Western liberal societies, is in radical decline. Unless there is a reversion to the ancient Tory view of the Constitution, in theory as well as in practice, with its adhesion to the Church on the grounds of its doctrinal purity, then the majority principle now operates so adversely to the Anglicans that no logical rationale exists for its persistence as a State Church. And, anyway, its doctrinal purity can only be discerned through the deployment of advanced imaginative faculties. The Church of England is not the kind of body you can grasp; as soon as you have, as you suppose, some purchase on what it purports to teach, you find the bit you hold has detached itself from the rest. In current circumstances of internal incoherence the Establishment of the Church of England is like the Establishment of a rather declassé debating society. The government fails to consult it about even the most portentous of ethical questions; instead it sets up 'ethical' advisory committees on which there sits, along with all the other token representatives of the plural society, a bishop or a professor of theology – nominated not in recognition of doctrinal orthodoxy but because of known liberal attitudes. At the basis of the Church Establishment is the parochial structure, the very presence of the 'national' Church in each locality, a visible sign that every citizen has the availability of spiritual service. It, too, is in decline. The strategy of locking up even this depleted ministry in these increasingly unrepresentative social units is plainly the wrong one. At its most fundamental level, in consequence, the Established Church has no real connection with national life. When it addresses the population on religious or moral issues few are inclined to be guided by the opinions or advice offered – unless, of course, these merely reflect their own conclusions, independently arrived at. In view of the close proximity of the clergy to the liberal, humanitarian beliefs of prevailing public opinion this last condition is sometimes achieved, but randomly. No one these days appears to look to the Church actually to teach Christian *doctrine:* it is ethical, and not spiritual, advice that they regard to be – if they regard anything to be – what the Establishment exists to provide in the life of the nation.

At this stage such considerations become merely matters of detail. The central question in the debate about Church and State relations ought to belong to the realm of Political Science. Does the modern liberal State in England have the philosophical capacity to recognize the truth of Christianity and to promote it as the confessional heart of its own existence? Does it have the will to do so, in the light of moral diversity among the population, of the defection of the intelligentsia from religious profession, of the probable collapse of the Church of England as a national institution, of the general organization of public life and of modern family life without reference to religion? The truth is that people today, if they bother with religious belief and practice at all, in any articulate sense, want to make up religious ideas for themselves. Religion has been largely privatized, and the Church is left with virtually no one to address. The State, having embraced humanist ethical values, even if in an anonymous form, and having declared its adhesion to a pluralistic understanding of the social nexus, is in practice anyway incapacitated from sponsoring the doctrinal structure of Christianity. In terms of political theory, the modern State, despite its ideological primitivism, has actually come to profess secular collectivist ideals, and enforces them. It is liberal dogmas, made increasingly illiberal through the extension of State regulation, which have replaced religious doctrine as the conscience of modern government.

It is immensely sad to have to witness the deconsecration of the State, the public admission that its purpose resides almost solely in relation to the material welfare of its citizens. The wise will shed a tear when the last prayers are offered in parliament, the last chaplains provided at the State's expense perform their duties in national institutions, the last religious observances take place in the schools, and the monarchy's sacral functions are removed from the constitutional process. Rather fewer may regret the expulsion of the bishops from the House of Lords. But the logic of Establishment has departed. The Church of England cannot even be a *symbol* of the nation's higher aspirations, for symbols are only effective if there is clarity and agreement about the ideas being symbolized. Sentiment does not become political reality unless it is sustained by political will. As for the secular State, it remains, according to traditional teaching and the exhortations of Saint Paul, a divine institution so long as it preserves order. Its ideas and practices, and the morality whose precepts it believes it expresses in its legislation, may be as benign or as hostile as were those which the State professed when the Church was founded. The first Christians recognized the legitimacy of the political order which sent them to their martyrdoms.

6

Indifferentism

There are breakers ahead for the Church of England on another issue too: interfaith worship is already above the surface as the tide reveals the full extent of the reef. There are still many of the older generations for whom the notion of *interdenominational* worship is a disagreeable novelty, and who could do without it: the concept of Moslems and Christians and Hindus worshipping together is going to prove a step too far. The issue is not about the exchange of courtesies and the extension of mutual respect, it must be remembered; nor is it merely an enlightened dialogue in which patent prejudices may be dispelled and devotees of each religion become informed. It is about addressing God in circumstances which suggest that one religion is as good as any other, and that it is God who is the same and people whose differences of view indicate merely cultural diversities and ethnic difference. Interfaith acts of worship really indicate human priorities, since the things that the worshippers have in common relate to matters of human self-esteem, and to ethicism. The idea of God becomes so generalized, in order to accommodate all the diverse understandings of him, that what is left is some sense of a vague spirit of benign intention to humanity – it is ethicism which is worshipped, the work of mens' hands, and not a divine person whose will for his creatures may clearly be discerned. He is made to be so universal and general as to have no particular form which can convey knowable truths. Not surprisingly, interfaith worship ends up worshipping the very means which were supposed only to be the way of celebrating God's glory – music, dance, artistic accomplishment, and so forth. These are festivals of humanity, celebrations of the key moral principle of the times: ethnic and cultural parity. Interfaith worship is multi-age and multi-class, appealing to the young who are prepared for the idea that one religion is as good as any other by modern school curriculae, and to the emissaries of higher thought, whose agnosticism can embrace religious sentiment only when it is divorced from discernable content. They think they are thinking for themselves: an understanding of religion which incorporates everything appears sophisticated. The appeal of the Ba'hai Faith to educated opinion is no mystery – its whole construction derives from an attempt to create a religion which includes all viewpoints. In fact it is probably the future of the Church of England. If the parish churches end up practising Ba'hai worship, and still calling it Anglicanism, it should surprise no one.

The error of believing that one religion is as good as any other was known in the nineteenth century as *Indifferentism*, and was wisely condemned as such – for being a universal dissolvent of faith – in Pius IX's

Syllabus of Errors in 1864. It was then the favoured religious ideal of liberals throughout Europe, whose dislike of the detailed formulations of Christianity in the historic Churches had not quite passed – as it has largely passed in our own day – into frank agnosticism. Separation from Catholicism appeared to be the badge of a thinker; explanation of the values to be encountered in other world religions coincided with advances both in anthropology and in the actual explorations of the countries remote from Europe which provided the data. Christianity was unworried by this shift in religious interest because it remained an academic and minority affair. Indeed, the relative resurgence in Christian confidence, associated with the political arrival of the middle classes, made the nineteenth century one of the great ages of missionary advance in the wider world. Off they went, to the furthest places, with their solar topees and their Prayer Books, to convert the natives. Now the ex-natives are building temples in Finsbury. Interfaith worship indicates not so much the sophistication of modern Christianity as its loss of confidence, its failure of nerve. It will prove to presage not a valuable new insight into the nature of God, but the eventual replacement of Christianity by atheism – in suitably understated expressions. But that is not the way it seems to those whose influence is uppermost in the Church of England.

There is, in the short-term, controversy over the matter. Interfaith worship is alien to the Evangelicals – not all of them – for whom the Revealed Truth of God is known with scripturally inspired precision.

And there are enough still left in the depleted Catholic wing of the Church whose sacramentalism is sufficiently explicit to disallow the notion of parity with pagan rites. For the liberals, however, who are driving the interfaith idea, enlightenment is falling like stars from the heavens. For here is the very embodiment of everything they have believed all along: a universalist religion without exact, or any, content, yet with precise ethical teaching based on concepts of Human Rights ideology. The celebrations themselves, the acts of worship, furthermore, are symbolical renditions of the current fad for cultural diversity, for social inclusion, for ethnic comprehension, and for human equality. This is the religion of the future, they believe – probably rightly. No longer will religious belief inspire violence and warfare as in the past; nor will it prove divisive inside civil society. A religion without a content builds readily from treating all the different religions as if they are all really the same. Religion which is so drained of doctrine that it is compatible with every other religion, that is so generalized as to be devoid of any possible cause of offence or misunderstanding, is so close to the modern practice of Anglicanism that its leaders will, in due time, be unable to resist it. The liberals are already there, beckoning the still unenlightened to the new utopia.

This religious relativism is the way of the future in Western societies, and the schools are in large measure to blame. Ever since the 1970s both Church schools and State schools have promoted a liberal agenda in relation to the content of religious education. The older concept of religious *instruction* has been abandoned in most of the Church schools: children are no longer encouraged in Christian doctrines, but are presented with choice. All the world religions are included in the curriculum, Christianity alongside the others, and children are left to decide their value for themselves. Current educational legislation provides that a preference should be given to the presentation of the Christian religion, but this is for reasons of national heritage and culture, and not because there is any intention to use the school curriculum to promote Christianity on the supposition of its inherent truth. In practice there is more or less complete parity in the manner in which the various faiths are taught. Indeed, there is a perceptible bias towards an uncritical explanation of religions like Hinduism, Buddhism and Islam, because the teachers are terrified of being accused of racism or cultural insensitivity; Christianity, in contrast, is generally conveyed as an ethical adjunct of current liberal issues in public morality, and its doctrinal basis is inadequately explained – if explained at all. What the children probably derive from all this is confusion, yet many doubtless persist in categorizing themselves as Christians: but this reflects family custom, and an equation of Christianity and benign ethicism, rather than conscious assent to doctrinal formulae. It is plain that children do not go to church; the Church is dying in England because it is failing to recruit a future membership. Modern intellectual culture encompasses the belief that mature people can make up a programme of religion for themselves, if that is their inclination. From the confused mixture of ideas and cultic practices which emerges from their years of school religious education, they are sewing together loose religious identities – when they bother to at all. In the nature of things these are described as 'Christianity', and account for the surprisingly high indications of surviving Christian belief in the findings of opinion polls. But they are not really Christian, since they are devoid of doctrinal content, rest on personal selections and preferences, have no institutional expression, are frequently associated with superstitious beliefs including communication with the dead, and are constructed according to individual selection. This is the version of the Faith which is brought to bear upon the new vogue of interfaith worship – as yet still a middle-class phenomenon, but soon to become widespread. In an age which distrusts discrimination of any kind, to be non-discriminatory in religion is a virtue.

Interfaith worship is growing in western countries. Though still in comparative infancy it is so clearly in sympathy with liberal culture that its future expansion seems secure. Step by step individual congregations are moving towards it, in well-intentioned attempts to promote inter-racial understanding and, for the liberals, as a means to devising a religion without doctrinal content. Because of its huge potential to provoke controversy within the Church the bishops are wary; many are plainly sympathetic to making some kind of endorsement of interfaith worship but will not do so until the climate becomes a little more favourable. Meanwhile, at parish level, and in individual cathedrals, the practice, in varying stages of coherent admission of what is going on, is becoming established. Grand State occasions held in major churches now conventionally incorporate an interfaith dimension. This began as ordinary courtesy, but has become a necessary part of the proceedings. It is civilized and proper; but it is sliding into the promotion of religious relativity when understood in the wider context of religious liberalism. The practice of interfaith worship is also a *Western* phenomenon. Where it is found in other parts of the world it is in large and Westernized urban areas (rather than in the countryside, where most people still live) and is among Westernized elites. In the West itself, and in England, interfaith worship represents the enthusiasm of articulate minorities in each of the religious groups involved. These groups are in current parlance referred to as 'faith communities', a politically correct designation, on the edge of receiving general usage, which itself promotes the concept of religious relativism. Each faith is as good as any other – this is what the expression signals – and because religion is to be thought of largely as a cultural matter a communal designation is appropriate in describing it.

There is also a widening gulf in English communities (and in the countries overseas which are their heartlands), between the manner in which the different religions are presented in interfaith exchanges and the practice of the religions themselves. This corresponds to the gap within Christianity, between the liberals and the folk religionists who call themselves

Christian, and the remaining minority who adhere, still, to traditional formulations of the Faith. There are sanitized, Westernized interpretations of Islam and Hinduism, for example, which are the ones presented to children in the schools. They derive from quite a long history of romanticizing the religions of the East, and of successful attempts by nineteenth-century colonial officials and Christian missionaries to secure the abolition of cruel or obscene rites. In order to make it clear that current British and American military interventions in Islamic states are not inspired by antipathy to Islam itself, British and American governmental agencies put out propaganda which fosters the idea of 'moderate' and acceptable Islam, quite unlike the 'extremism' of the 'fundamentalists'. These same fundamentalists, however, constitute the larger part of Islam throughout the world, and their religion is not fanatical or extremist – it is simply the political and cultural embodiment of doctrinal propositions, the sort of thing which formed the normal aspirations of Christendom for the best part of two thousand years. There are plenty of secular Moslems, as there are secular Jews and enormous numbers of secular Christians. 'Islam', as presented by Western liberals and by the Westernized elites among the Islamic leadership in Western countries, is not secular in this sense, however; it is a new interpretation of the Faith, manufactured in order to be compatible with Western democratic practices and liberal ideals. This is the version of Islam which enters the interfaith worship encounters, and there are comparable artefacts made from Buddhism,

Hinduism and even Judaism – Christianity's parent body.

Nobody seems bothered about determining where the line is drawn for inclusion. Should interfaith worship invite *all* the religions found in the world? The religion of the aboriginals of Australia is now widely admired for its supposedly sophisticated insights into the nature of things: should this version of animism take its place alongside Catholicism and Orthodoxy? And what of the cultic practices of the Amazonian tribes, or the religious customs of the Papuans? At this point the prevalent inclination to politically correct cultural relativism embraces relativism in religion, and it is merely human attributes and values which prevail. Religion is becoming a celebration of humanity, not the acknowledgement of the sovereignty of God at all. It is not really because the 'God' worshipped by all the diverse components who participate in the interfaith exchanges is the same God – it is because it is the same *humanity* that takes part: that is what matters to the enthusiasts of these enterprises. Just as the concept of 'spirituality' has been secularized, and is now used to indicate merely human reflective instincts, so 'religion' now signals, it would seem, any understanding of a first cause or moving spirit which sustains the phenomenon of humanity. 'Not everyone who says Lord, Lord, shall enter the Kingdom of Heaven', Jesus said, 'but he who does the will of any Father who is in Heaven' (Matthew 7.21). Modern liberals redefine the 'will' of God within such generously extended parameters as to render these words virtually meaningless. Interfaith worship is the celebration of their mistaken generosity.

The Christian religion rests upon Revelation. God, it is true, had disclosed his presence through the works of his creation – the universe itself, and this planet, upon which he placed a humanity endowed with sufficient capacities of reason and reflexion as to be able to discern his presence. Hence Natural Religion; but it intimates only a latent knowledge of God – the divine sensed through the materials of his creation. The different religions of the world each express this sense in the symbols and images appropriate to their various cultural developments. The Jewish tradition of understanding, too, took its origins through a God of fire and thunder. But God had willed that he was to be known about explicitly: the latency or implicit disclosure was a universal preparation of humanity, and not a sufficiency in what was to be humanity's highest vocation – to participate with God in the development of the earth, and to become, through obedience and service, immortal creatures. When God revealed himself in Jesus Christ, the universal creator of all things became himself a particular being in the full nature of material things, whilst remaining, still, fully divine. The message he then conveyed to his creatures was made in the manner prepared in Natural Religion: through actual and real events in existing society. Modern people prefer religion to be general and vaguely defined, to be incorporate and indiscriminate in its benign purposes. Jesus, however, was concerned with the particular and the concrete, with

speaking through the particular culture of a particular people at a particular time. Thus his message was
knowable because it was addressed within an exact
context. He did not offer a system of ideas or a philosophy – the general – but spoke to particular humans
in particular situations – a message of salvation
entrusted to people. That people is the Church of
Christ, which Jesus set up in his own lifetime when
he trained and sent out followers to preach in the
towns around him. The religion of Jesus is a direct
Revelation of God's nature, known precisely and
exactly by humans because it was given directly
to them – not in some symbol, or magical event, or
through the understanding of an interlocutor or
prophet. When God speaks, in Jesus, the knowledge
conveyed is all truth, not a partial version of it, and
the person from whom the utterances are made is
owed all obedience, not a conditional assent. How do
Christians know that their religion is true? It is
because God founded it directly himself. Where do
they look today for an interpretation of that truth in
the appropriate vocabulary of the times? To the
people who for two thousand years have been the tradition of belief – to the Church. A religion that rests
upon Revelation is able to make unique claims to
authenticity. Interfaith *dialogue* is to be encouraged
since it may eliminate misunderstandings and culti-
vate social harmony; interfaith *worship* is a contradiction in terms, since you cannot worship a God who
is so imprecisely known that he is compatible with
the exclusive claims actually made in many religions,
and certainly in Christianity. If each worshipper, in

these celebrations, retains his own understanding of God, whilst seeming to worship alongside others from other traditions of belief who have quite contrary ideas, there is equivocation and denial of the unique calling which is central to Christianity. Modern enthusiasts for interfaith enterprises should examine the ministry of Jesus, which was sometimes important for what he did not say. And among the things he did not say was that all religions were of equal value. There would not have been much point in God making a particular revelation of himself had that been the case. He sent his followers out to teach all nations. What would he have made of the modern Anglican disinclination to proselytize among adherents of other faiths? How would he have assessed the current taste for regarding primitive dream-interpreters among desert tribes as equal to celebrations of the Mass? 'What man is there of you', Jesus said, 'who if his son asks for bread will give him a stone?' (Matthew 7.10). And on another occasion: 'Strive to enter in at the straight gate, for many, I say to you, will seek to enter in and shall not be able' (Luke 13.24). The claims of Christ *are* exclusive; there is no other way of interpreting the simple meaning of his words. All religions are *not* of equal value, and as Anglicanism drifts towards public celebrations which appear to suggest that they are, its demise as a distinctively Christian body will draw closer. This is a matter just opening up now, and which doubtless will provoke controversy. Hence the determination of the leadership not to see the question formally discussed in the central bodies of the Church. It is better, they must be calculating, to turn a blind eye to the drift towards interfaith worship presently taking place than to initiate further controversy.

7

The crisis of authority in the Church: 1. Causes

❧

The Church was not founded at Pentecost, as is sometimes said, but by Christ during the course of his ministry in Galilee and Judea. It was he who appointed the twelve to become what today, perhaps, would be called teaching officers, and who commissioned the seventy as a *corps* of evangelistic missioners. In the ancient world religious knowledge was sometimes committed to sacred writings, sometimes to a school of ideas, sometimes to a priestly caste or an assemblage of cultic observances, and sometimes it emerged episodically through the translations of oracles. Christ, in contrast, revealed his truth to a living company of people – 'the People of God' – who, after his corporeal departure became his body on earth. Precisely because the message was thus conveyed organically it remained permanently new: able to adapt to changing intellectual modes and social filtration, capable of bringing forward fresh insights in the successive cultural shifts of a progressive humanity. Written texts do not transmit truth of themselves: they require reinterpretation, over long periods of time, if they are to achieve durable meaning. Priestly castes have the disadvantage of

101

imploding into small coteries of exclusivity; they frequently become a mere adjunct of ruling elites. Philosophical systems tend to die when the surrounding culture to which they originally related transforms itself or disintegrates. But a living body of people, at the centre of whose religious insights is not a set of ideas but a person, has the verifiable capability of enduring through the centuries, forever changing yet forever the same.

In the essentials of its historical conveyance of Christ, furthermore, this people must be as indefectible as he is, not only because the Church is *actually* his body, but because Christ himself, in the gift of the Holy Spirit, promised perpetual guidance into all truth. Whatever the apostles were commissioned to do the Church today has the authority to do. After the first two hundred years the successors of the apostles drew up a new canon of sacred writings: the authority they exercised to determine which sacred literature (the New Testament) was to be recognized is still resident in the Church. The teaching office of the Church, the *Magisterium,* precedes the written Gospels and remains as the dynamic of the Christian mission. It is embodied in 'tradition', the succession of authentic representation of Christ carried through human cultures by those who seek obedience to Christ's first calling. The Church is often thought of today as primarily a kind of fellowship, a collective therapy which exists to assist human emotional need. It may indeed have some qualities which attach to those features but the Church is actually and overwhelmingly an institutionalized teaching office. Hence the importance of its vitality: as an organism it can adapt and grow, it can sever limbs which become diseased, it can show inventive genius. Its infallibility in essentials provides a permanent standard and a point of stability; its errors in contingent matters are the corrosions of the world, the humanity which produces flaws in the operation of all institutions – even when they are perfect in authority. Because it is organic the Church can make 'developments' of doctrine. Over time some features of Christ's truth may require to be accorded more significance than others, or advances in knowledge and changes in culture may re-cast the manner in which the mysteries of religion are formulated. The Church can never invent or create doctrines, but it can define or declare them, with images appropriate to circumstance, so that truths implicit in the understanding of the first believers may only over centuries assume richer meaning. The smallest of seeds becomes the mustard plant; there is no way initially of telling which dimensions of Christ's teaching may assume importance in the history of society. It is a sign of the authority of Christ in his Church that the People of God are capable of defining the nature of his presence in contexts that are unavoidably transient. 'Development' of doctrine, as associated, for example, with St Vincent of Lerins, or with Franzelin or Newman, has proved controversial because to Protestants actual cases in the last couple of centuries have concerned issues, like the place of the Virgin in the scheme of salvation, and the centralization of the infallible office of the Church itself, for which they have had limited enthusiasm. But the key idea that a living Church can, as Christ's body, continue to unfold the mysteries of the Kingdom is not in itself controversial. Most Christians have always believed it. Development occurs within the promise of the Holy Spirit's guidance, as within the standard of Scripture, and the teaching tradition of the successors of the apostles: 'Sacred Tradition; Sacred Scripture and the Magisterium of the Church are so connected and associated that one of them cannot stand without the others', as the *Catechism of the Catholic Church* expresses it.

The infallible essentials are recognized by their consistency in the universal declaration of the People of God: the teaching that is made everywhere and at all times, the *sensus fidei*. Occasionally, and since the earliest times, controverted points of doctrine have required clarification, and for this the people have gathered in General Councils and elicited, by their *consensus fidelium,* the mind of Christ. For this, plainly, unity is a necessary condition, and a test for the existence of ecclesiastical authenticity has been the continued integration of each local Church with the communion originally instituted by the apostles. In Augustine's phrase – the definition which so pulverized Newman's understanding of the Anglican claim to be the *Via Media* – 'Quapropter securus judicat orbis terrarum, bonos non esse qui se devidunt ab orbe terrarum.' [Wherefore, the entire world judges with security that they are not good who separate themselves from the entire world.] It is therefore to General Councils that those who stand in the tradition of the historic Churches look for infallible teaching, but only to supplement the pre-existing deposit of received truth. The authority of the Church does not derive from legal conditions like the regularity of orders – important though they may be for other reasons – but from what is actually being taught at any time, and from showing that this body of teaching corresponds with what is being taught universally.

The problem with a 'Doctrine of the Church' is in determining how 'the People of God' may be identified when there exists, as there has virtually always existed, a division within Christianity. This is compounded by the insistence of some Protestants, in the last five centuries, that *no* Church is possessed of an indefectible body of teaching, anyway, and that the commission of Christ is in reality distributed to a number of different traditions, some of which, though entirely national and local – as the Church of England was before its extension overseas – claim to be self-sufficient in Christian understanding. Christian believers in this condition have sought to establish their authenticity by reference to Scripture. The difficulty here is that the authority of Scripture derives from the body which selected and canonized it: the Church. A further difficulty is that nineteenth-century scholarship (historical and anthropological as much as theological) has rather compromised the reliability and integrity of Scripture as an infallible resource. It is also awkward for Protestants to argue consistency of teaching since they do not agree among themselves over an impressively wide range of points, and in the case of the Church of England these disagreements extend internally across the whole understanding of its adherents. Most of these disagreements, it is true, are over matters of order, discipline and liturgical practice, rather than doctrine; and over the Doctrine of the Church itself there is little disagreement since Protestantism is recognized by the imprecision of the language and images currently used in substitution of having a coherent Doctrine of the Church at all.

Most Anglicans are unaware that there is a problem over the Church's ecclesiology. Probably most members of the clergy have scarcely concerned themselves with the matter: certainly the kind of teaching available in ministerial and theological training today does not raise issues of this sort with any noticeable profundity. Sermons preached in order to promote Christian unity, for example, almost never include the Doctrine of the Church itself as among the reasons for disunity – yet it is the greatest stumbling block in ecumenism. The matter is, however, absolutely crucial: the question of authority – of the means by which truth is known to be true – is the very basis of all religious association. If sacred writings could stand independently of time and circumstance, if they could speak, as it were, for themselves, there would be some mitigation. But texts require exposition and explanation; the cultural assumptions which determined the manner in which the information they convey was established have to be interpreted. It is the living Church which does this, and the process is a creative one. The body which in the first place distinguished which texts carried authentic truth about

Christ and which were corrupted by, for example, folk miracles or miraculous fantasies (and there were plenty of them circulating in the first two centuries), is still called upon to deploy its gifts of indefectibility to extricate the person of Christ from the written word. It is the last claim, made by the historic Churches, which Anglicans appear to deny. In its scepticism about the infallible office of the universal Church, Anglicanism is unavoidably Protestant in character, however much of historic doctrine it may otherwise have retained faithfully, and however attentive it has been to regularity in episcopal ordination. The historic Doctrine of the Church, which it rejected at the time of the Reformation, is the one which defines authority. Anglicans have not yet decided upon a substitute.

Though most Anglicans are unaware of the problem, a few have recognized its gravity, often as a consequence of exchanges made with ecumenical intent. The usual route to the problem, however, has been through the Anglican pursuit of an identity – in its, at times, almost frenetic quest for some ground of unity. 'Anglican apologists,' Bishop Stephen Sykes noticed in 1978, 'have not always seen that their attempts to explain how all the various viewpoints coexist in one communion raise extremely far-reaching issues about the nature of the Church.' That was in his *Integrity of Anglicanism,* a work which, as Dr William Sachs remarked in amplification of his own observation that 'uncertainty about the Church's identity has reached crisis proportions', had since the 1970s 'framed the debate's contours'. Writing in the

context of the Lambeth Conference of 1988, J. Robert
Wright, Professor of Ecclesiastical History at the
General Theological Seminary in New York City,
affirmed that 'as far as the taking of authoritative
decisions is concerned, there is clearly a vacuum at
the centre, whether one chooses to evaluate it posi-
tively or negatively'. This is true both in point of
jurisdiction and in relation to the interpretation of
doctrine. The Doctrine Commission of the Church of
England appointed by the Archbishops of Canterbury
and York in 1922 (which reported in 1938) itself had
no consideration of the Doctrine of the Church as
such, but was addressed to the pervasive difficulty of
Anglican unity: 'It was not appointed in order to
survey the whole field of theology and produce a
systematic treatise,' the Commissioners admitted;
'The Commission was appointed because the tensions
between different schools of thought in the Church of
England were imperilling its unity.' Its explanation of
many doctrinal propositions was unquestionably
useful; about the document as a whole, however, there
hung a distinctive Anglican atmosphere of indecision
over fundamentals. Thus 'On Assent' the Commissioners laid out seven resolutions 'with a view to the
avoidance of misunderstanding'. The sixth, and most
important, declared that 'if any authorized teacher
puts forward personal opinions which diverge . . .
from the traditional teaching of the Church, he should
be careful to distinguish between such opinions and
the normal teaching which he gives in the Church's
name'. Attached to the resolution, however, was a
note pointing out that some members of the Commis-

sion 'while not dissenting from these resolutions' proceeded to do exactly that. The Report of the Doctrine Commission of 1976 demonstrated the same phenomenon at more considered length: the substantive findings covered forty-two pages and the dissenting and alternative explanations, a hundred and fourteen.

'The authority of the Church in the realm of doctrine arises from its commission to preach the Gospel to all the world' – the words are those of the 1938 Report – 'and the promises, accompanying that commission, that the Lord would always be with his disciples, and that the Holy Spirit would guide them into all the truth'. It is an admirable summary. But what is the institutional translation? Anglicans have not been backward in recognizing that they have a problem of identity. The debate had once turned on Anglicanism as a middle course between the historic Churches and non-episcopal Protestantism; statements of fundamentals, like the Lambeth Quadrilateral of 1888 (itself echoing the preceding Chicago formula of 1886) had demonstrated a reductionism which avoided the basic difficulty of defining an institutional source of authority. That most of the European Protestant Churches had retained a historic so-called 'deposit' of faith was not really in question. Even Pusey, in his reliance on the concept of such a deposit to defend Catholic aspects of Anglicanism at the time of the Gorham Case in 1850, did not place its origins in a living tradition of teaching, however, but in Scripture. The Lambeth Conferences have all been concerned essentially with the retention of unity: but

without a coherent Doctrine of the Church the participants have recurringly experienced fearful difficulty
in defining how the evident diversities within Anglicanism are compatible with the singularity of authority necessarily inseparable from the body of Christ in
the world. Unity and authority are not quite the same
thing – for there are a number of ways legitimately to
signal unity – but they are plainly very closely related
to virtually all the practical tests it is possible to
propose. Anglicans once supposed themselves united
by adhesion to Scripture, but Scriptural authority, as
already pointed out, does not convey the same implications today as it did in, say, the seventeenth
century, before the consequences of critical scholarship began to dissolve away old certainties. The
Prayer Book was also a badge of unity, but most
Anglicans younger than middle age have probably
never seen one. The Thirty-nine Articles of Religion,
which represent a selection of contentious issues as
they presented themselves in the sixteenth century,
are sometimes characterized not only as ambiguous –
which they certainly are – but as redundant. 'I rather
think of them as a kind of monument to an attempt on
our part, centuries ago, to show how far we could go
in the direction of a confessional attitude without
actually adopting one,' said Bishop Stephen Bayne, in
1964, at the end of his period as Executive Officer of
the Anglican Communion. 'In any case,' he added,
'they are museum pieces now.' Bishop Bayne's office,
not surprisingly, was itself unofficial, since there is,
in Anglicanism, no mechanism for creating offices
with pan-Anglican authority. Here is his considered

summary of Anglican attempts at defining a basis of unity:

> We have no particular theological statement of our own to fence us off from other Churches. We have no international power structure which forces our younger Churches to conform to some alien pattern of life. We have no central executive power. We have no uniform Prayer Book. We have no common language. We have no laws which limit the freedom of any Church to decide its life as it will. We have no ecclesiastical colonies. We have no 'Anglican' religion. We have no test of membership save that of Baptism itself. We have nothing to hold us together except the one essential unity given us in our full communion. And even that is not limited to Anglican Churches, for we share in the table of other Churches as well, in increasing number.

The last point is extremely important. For the expansion of ecumenical courtesies in the second half of the twentieth century has allowed Anglicanism the illusion of seeing itself as part of a wider context of Christian unity. The reality is actually that the participant Churches in such arrangements each retain their differences, including decisively different understandings of the nature of authority itself, and therefore of the Doctrine of the Church. These measures of intercommunion are not moves towards Christian unity, especially since the historic

Churches, who *do* have distinct ecclesiologies, are largely outside them; they are moves towards a sort of loose federalism in which spiritual camaraderie is mistaken for structural agreement about identifying who the People of God are.

Anglicans who rely on the existence of an authentic priestly ministry are not really helped either. The technical line of Apostolical succession and regular ordination procedures may or may not have been preserved within the Church of England, and passed to the subsequent lateral Churches, but it scarcely matters when it comes to determining the capacity to order doctrine. The whole issue was clouded by the priority given to the question of episcopal ordination at the Savoy Conference in 1661, and then, in the nineteenth century, by the Tractarians, in their hurried belief that the authenticity of a Catholic identity for the Church of England could be recovered by proving an episcopal succession. This itself had simply revealed, once again, how varied were the opinions held within Anglicanism, for it had not mattered to most of the leadership before. The absence of any abiding sense that Anglicanism was anchored in apostolic orders was revealed, for example, in 1817 when a Church of England minister (A. B. Johnson) was appointed for Sierra Leone by the Church Missionary Society: he was ordained by Lutheran pastors. And the row over the Jerusalem bishopric in 1841 indicated how little the matter of regularity in episcopal jurisdiction depended on a Catholic pedigree. Overseas bishops – the very foundation of most of what became the worldwide

Anglican Communion – were until 1864 named by the Colonial Office under Letters Patent. In 1992 the Church of England agreed a common membership with five Nordic and three Baltic Lutheran Churches, at Porvoo: this created a single interchangeable ministry. Not all of the Churches involved had preserved episcopal ordination continuously. The fact is that, in the historic tradition of Western Christianity, as in the early Church, it is not regularity of ordination that guarantees authenticity but what those who are ordained actually teach; ordination or consecration does not in itself convey *jurisdiction* – or the means of safeguarding doctrinal purity. Those who fall into heresy, after all, have generally been led by properly ordained clergy in full apostolic succession. It is not how the leadership acquires its charisms which is relevant in the issue of authority, but how the People of God as a whole is to be identified. The test of authentic teaching is not that it comes from a personage ordained in a certain prescribed manner, but that it is in correspondence with what is being taught throughout the worldwide body of Christ.

Problems of identity, unity and authority, were not solved, and sometimes were not specifically addressed, by the expansion of the Church of England overseas. The 'Anglican Communion' – an expression first used in 1851 – is simply a number of autonomous bodies which exactly reproduce the same problems of identity as the parent Church. They are united in having had, in different legal conditions, to redefine their relationship to host political communities as a consequence of the constitutional separations of

Church and State made, in the case of America in the eighteenth century, and elsewhere in the nineteenth. The abandonment of 'national' Church status has helped, rather than impeded, their capacity to be categorized as potential candidates for universality, whatever disadvantages may have accompanied disestablishment. There are problems about the concept of a 'national' Church, as the Church of England, which still is one, knows only too well. At the time of the Donatist heresy, early in the fifth century, Optatus denied that any 'national' Church could be a reliable custodian of universal truth. The body of Christ is committed to the entirety of peoples, and the witness of the entire world (unity, that is to say) affords the test of authenticity. Christ's body is indivisible, and it does not allow of national characteristics except in accidental features and contingent applications. This was true in relation to the relatively multicultural circumstances of the Hellenistic, Roman and Byzantine worlds, and it is certainly true today, when national self-consciousness is determined by post-Romantic nationalism. The Jewish nation was chosen by God and incarnated certain truths about his operations in human society; but the whole point about the history of Israel is that it was the *education* of a people. Once brought to completion in Christ the whole revelation of God was universalized, and Jew and gentile, male and female, free and slave, were recognized as being a single people. The Church obviously takes on the cultural characteristics of successive ages, and in turn influences them, yet the Church is essentially outside national possession,

particularly since the word 'national' has so many resonances and such various applications. The idea of a
'national' Church is probably a contradiction in terms.
'Establishment' of the Church by the State is, paradoxically almost, a separate matter. The Catholic
Church, that most universal of Christian institutions,
has been, and still is, 'established' by constitutional
provision or explicit legal protection in a number of
countries. This indicates the State, which Christians
have always considered a divine institution, recognizing and promoting the Christian religion at the centre
of its moral identity. It is completely compatible with
spiritual autonomy: that depends on the terms of
association agreed between Church and State. In the
case of England's erastian polity, since the Reformation, it is a matter of judgement whether spiritual
autonomy was preserved. Parliament became the
effective governing body of the Church. The Tractarians, reflecting an older tradition of Anglican divines,
always maintained that this was compatible with
spiritual autonomy so long as parliament could be
estimated to be an assembly of the Church's laity. The
real test of spiritual autonomy, however, is the
capacity of a Church to conform to the universality of
the whole Church – and that was, and is, denied by
the existence of the Royal Supremacy in religion. To
be spiritually autonomous the Church must show
that, as the organic body of Christ, it has the capacity
to determine truth from error; that it is possessed of a
Doctrine of the Church. The modern growth of
ecclesiastical autonomy has not solved the problem: it
has merely removed some anomalies in the day-to-day

conduct of the Church as an institution. The matura-
tion of the worldwide Anglican Communion, similarly,
did not solve the problem. Anglicans sometimes speak
as if the sheer scale of the Communion as a whole is a
sort of proof that they are part of a truly universal
Church. Yet a universal Church in the sense meant by
Augustine and the Fathers did not derive its authentication from mere numbers, but from consistency of
teaching. There are many indications in the words of
Christ himself which suggest that he considered that
the numbers of his real followers, in all societies,
would always be small. The Anglican Communion has
universalized the Anglican pursuit of an identity as a
Church; it has not qualitatively made any difference
to the ingredients of the problems of ecclesiology. And
the considerable cultural diversity it now shows is a
by-product of historical development, not evidence of
inherent universality.

The whole idea of the Anglican Communion did not
relate to models of universality taken from Antiquity,
nor was it derived from the writings of the Fathers. It
was not even put together with any consciousness of
adducing or embodying a Doctrine of the Church. It
appeared by chance. It was modelled, in fact, on the
simultaneous evolution of the British Commonwealth
of Nations, and developed out of a very incoherent
theory of empire. The preceding separations of
Church and State were not brought about (as
Anglicans, especially High Church Anglicans, liked to
suppose) because, through the experience of mission,
churchmen rediscovered the spiritual autonomy of the
Church. They did indeed make that discovery, but

only after the State had decided to discontinue government financial assistance – and that did not come because of any prior secularization of the colonial administration, but because the State in the colonies, as it developed through 'responsible government' to national political autonomy, encountered the hard facts of denominational pluralism – just as it was beginning to do inside the United Kingdom itself in the nineteenth century. It shed its ecclesiastical functions because a majority of its citizens were no longer potential beneficiaries, and rather forcibly pointed this out.

The religious autonomy which necessarily followed was rendered in the form of synods. The first examples were in the new American states, with their arrangement of conventions, and of the national Episcopal Convention of 1785. These were frankly modelled on the secular representative instruments of government which came into existence in the Republic generally, and they had lay participation. The intention was not to embody a Doctrine of the Church, but to secure participation and to regularize ecclesiastical appointments. In the countries of the British Empire, comparably, the growth of synods followed secular models of contemporaneous constitutional experiment. Bishop George Augustus Selwyn's seminal gathering in New Zealand in 1844, and Bishop William Broughton's provincial synod in 1850, led the way. Synods, in the history of the Church, do not determine doctrine, and have only local authority; and that was the case with the Anglican revivals. Their purpose was the exercise of order and ecclesiastical jurisdiction on a voluntary basis, not the determination of truth. It was in the practice of these functions that High Churchmen began to dream of religious authority as it had been before the erastianism of the English Reformation: it was then that mission conditions breathed new life into Catholic Anglicanism, and its Zephirus came from Oxford. But they recognized that the synods as such were not substitutes for General Councils of the Church, could certainly not claim indefectibility (as Councils could not either, in Anglican discernment), and were essentially bodies to regularize decisions in questions of order and discipline. Selwyn described his first synod as intended 'to frame rules for the better management of the mission and general government of the Church'. As it spread, however, synodical government encountered opposition from Evangelicals and Erastians, fearful of clerical aggrandizement and departure from the sovereign authority of Scripture. They need not have worried. Synodical government was discussed at the first Lambeth Conference in 1867 and endorsed in a compromise resolution actually proposed by Selwyn, which referred to the 'due and canonical subordination of the synods of the several branches to the higher authority of a synod or synods above them'. Since no such higher synods existed, nor was there any means of convening them, this was the ideal Anglican formula. It was without meaning.

The English Convocations of Canterbury and York were provincial synods under another name, but their deliberative functions were suspended between 1717 and 1852 (and 1862). Convocations were never regarded as appropriate places for the determination of doctrine, and even Francis Atterbury in his defence of the spiritual integrity of Convocation against the erastianism of Archbishop William Wake, in the dispute of 1697, did not attribute a doctrinal role to them. There was a disorientating moment in 1538, immediately after the Reformation statutes, when a synod of English clergy was convened to discuss the nature of the sacraments – certainly a doctrinal matter. But it was called by Thomas Cromwell, using secular authority, and its powers over doctrine were left undefined. Preceding synods, which of course did not have the capacity to determine doctrine either, had been summoned by legatine authority.

What of the authority of Lambeth Conferences? As a source of doctrinal definition they can easily be eliminated from the quest, since they have disclaimed any such authority from the start. Bishop John Henry Hopkins of Vermont, later Presiding Bishop of the Episcopal church, and a scholar fully informed about the procedures of the early Church, had in 1851 suggested an Anglican General Council, but neither he, nor subsequent exponents of some kind of international body, envisaged the determination of doctrine as among its powers. The English bishops, operating within a persistent atmosphere of erastianism, had anyway to be extremely cautious of any clerical assembly which exercised effective powers independently of statute law. At the start of the first Lambeth Conference in 1867 Archbishop Longley made it clear that the gathering was a conference and not a synod, and that its resolutions would be purely declaratory –

they would have only the influence of recommendations. That has remained the position to this day: the
resolutions of Lambeth Conferences only have effect if
enacted by synods in each constituent Church of the
Communion. The 1862 Conference did in fact recom-
mend the creation of what it termed 'a voluntary
spiritual Tribunal', with representatives from each
Anglican province, 'to secure unity in matters of faith
and uniformity in matters of discipline'. This never
came to pass; had it done so its 'voluntary' character
would anyway have incapacitated its potential to
evolve into a source of doctrinal authority. The
nearest the Church of England has come to an effective exercise of authority in a matter of doctrine was
when Archbishop Runcie proposed, in a brief and
indecisive debate in the General Synod, that the
doctrine of the Double Procession of the Holy Spirit
should be deleted from the Nicene Creed. The Provincial Synod of the South African Church had done this
in 1982. The General Synod in England is plainly not
a body with the appropriate authority to determine
doctrine, yet the Double Procession has disappeared
from the Creed in *Common Worship*. The idea, similarly, of the See of Canterbury being recognized as the
universal Patriarchate of the Anglican Communion,
proposed by Selwyn in the 1870s, and subsequently
raised in a number of Lambeth Conferences, has not
found acceptance. This is wise: the title of patriarch is
not a mere courtesy, and carries distinct inferences of
precedence and jurisdiction which are incompatible
with the notion of the Anglican Communion as a voluntary association. It does not realistically compare

with the autocephalous status of Churches within Orthodoxy, and certainly not with the Latin Patriarchate of Rome. Until fairly recent times it could also be pointed out that the Church of England was not in communion with any other Churches – apart from its own colonial relatives. Modern ecumenical arrangements have altered this situation, but only marginally: the participants of intercommunion agreements are all Protestant. This is not a step towards a greater reunion of Christianity, in fact, since the basic issue of authority remains unaddressed; the constituents of intercommunion are united by *not* believing in the doctrine of an infallible teaching office. All the Protestant intercommunions have achieved, to be starkly realistic, is a further polarization of those who hold to the existence of an authority and those who do not.

8

The crisis of authority in
the Church: 2. Effects

❧

Anglicans have always considered themselves to be
both the inheritor of medieval Christianity in
England, the legitimate succession to the mission
established by Augustine of Canterbury, and also a
'branch' of the universal Church. In this version of
ecclesiology 'the Church' comprises all recognized
Christian bodies, divided by location and tradition.
But recognized by whom? To what sort of sliding-scale
is it possible to refer to determine whether a particular Church conveys authentic Christian truth? Does
the definition, for example, include only Trinitarian
Christians? The World Council of Churches, for its
part, appears to operate a policy of practical coopera-
tion between the various affiliated bodies without
enquiring into their doctrinal orthodoxy. How is it
possible to recognize heretical Churches from those
which adhere to apostolic teaching? Does the Anglican
Communion regard itself as a constituent of a
'Church' which is so broadly defined as to have no
precise doctrinal content apart from subscription to
the authority of the Scriptures? Since the basic
division within Christianity corresponds to positions
adopted in relation to the question of indefectible

teaching, it is difficult to conceive a definition of the universal Church which includes all viewpoints. The entire metaphor of 'branches' is difficult to apply and as used by Christ himself, when he said 'I am the vine, you are the branches', it had a clearly discriminatory intent. 'As the branch cannot bear fruit of itself, unless it abide in the vine, so neither can you unless you abide in me.' The universal Church is the united body of Christ; there is no other definition.

The branch theory fits very well with the concept of 'dispersed authority', which will be considered shortly, and evidently regards the 'Church', as a concept, as constituted from diverse and mutually conflicting understandings of Christ's teaching, held together – or, rather, patently *not* held together – by simply calling themselves parts of a greater yet undefined entity.

The test of subscription to the inerrancy of Scripture is no longer an unambiguous possibility for the authentication of Christian teaching. The manner in which the scriptural texts are received and interpreted – which has in reality always changed, from the florid allegories and symbolism employed by the early Fathers, to the literalism of some modern Evangelicals – can no longer allow simple acceptance. It was an extraordinary irony that the scholars at the time of the Reformation who sought a return to the exclusive authority of Holy Scripture were also the ones whose very scholarship had revealed how insecure the texts were, when they subjected the verbal accuracy of the Vulgate to extensive critical analysis. Nineteenth century modes of Biblical understanding inaugurated a theological culture which has left the notion of scriptural inerrancy problematical to say the least. The idea that only those Christian doctrines and moral practices are essential which may be found in Scripture, which is the Anglican position (Article VI), is compatible with modern Biblical criticism but rests upon a restricted understanding of revelation, an implied denial of Development, and a refusal to contemplate the survival of the original magisterium conferred by Christ to his followers. If the fullness of the Christian revelation must be authenticated exclusively in relation to Scripture, there will be an enormous problem when, in the future, really dramatic shifts in the general culture require truly radical restatements of the Faith.

Liturgy has sometimes been considered an authoritative means for the Church to witness to its essential beliefs, and indeed this used to be so. Yet there are problems here, too, wrought by historical change. Orthodoxy has committed truth to liturgical forms, and to alter the liturgy, therefore, would compromise truth itself. In the Western Church, however, worship has been changed many times, and although alterations of style and even of liturgical images may not of themselves effect the doctrinal truths conveyed they do not allow liturgy, as such, to be judged a secure guarantee of doctrinal authenticity. The liturgical practices of the Church of England at the present time, for example, are determined by committees of expert liturgists who do not, for obvious reasons, wield the authority imparted by General

Councils. Liturgical use can only transmit teaching: it cannot help resolve fundamental difficulties if the means of determining truth are controverted in the first place.

Anglicans have always sought to overcome problems about their inability to accept the unitary nature of the teaching found within the historic Churches by distinguishing between 'essentials' and 'inessentials'. The tradition, reinforced by Melanchton during the Reformation, articulated the distinction – which was, indeed, familiar enough in the speculative thought of the Hellenistic Fathers. The number of items in the *adiaphora* list, however, has grown in proportion to the multiplication of divergencies inside the Church of England. The Catholics, in contrast, have held to the position that all doctrines, once determined, are equally true but are arranged in a hierarchy of importance which may alter with circumstance. It is difficult to see how these two positions are compatible without either the Anglicans redefining their source of authority or the Catholics restricting theirs. The fact is that there is not, as Anglicans suppose, a single 'deposit' of faith inherited from Antiquity, but a range of rival understandings about the means of authenticating the ingredients of the deposit. Hence the difficulty about General Councils. At the time of the Reformation there was a broad agreement among both those who remained in the Catholic Church and those who separated themselves, that Councils were the proper means of determining doctrine. The immediate problem was to whom belonged the authority to summon a Council. The early Church offered examples of gatherings called both exclusively by bishops and exclusively by civil authorities. Anti-papal sentiment in sixteenth-century Europe, and the contemporaneous aggrandizement of monarchy, hedged both propositions with what turned out to be insuperable barriers. It was a question of the Pope's authority as the embodiment of the indefectible magisterium of the Church *versus* a divided political order. The matter in the end proved academic, since Protestants – and the Church of England with them – came to deny the infallibility of conciliar definitions of essential points of faith and morals. And here is a fundamental issue at the centre of the Anglican pursuit of authority. Article XXI (1571) insists that General Councils 'may not be gathered together without the command and will of Princes'; and that 'they may err, and sometimes have erred, even in things pertaining unto God'. The last phrase is significant because it suggests essential matters, the very 'deposit' of faith indeed. The point about the sanction of the civil authority is equally awkward: the subsequent historical separation of sacred and secular in political society has rendered it inoperable throughout virtually every part of the Anglican Communion – except, potentially, within the Church of England itself, which still is, at time of writing, established by law, and with the relevant 'Prince' as its Supreme Governor. No one, presumably, is going to imagine it appropriate that the British sovereign will ever convene a General Council. The Catholic Church, which periodically does meet in General Council, last faced the intervention of the

Powers at the first Vatican Council in 1870; the threat then proved empty, and by the time of the Second Vatican Council it was unthinkable. Anglican teaching maintains that the declarations of Councils are only binding if they are in conformity with Scripture, though this notion can hardly have applied to the conciliar declaration of the canon of scripture itself, for nowhere in the Bible is the authority of the Bible declared. It is also unclear why Anglicans need have a view about Councils at all. Since they have no practical means of convening one, and no qualification to attend one summoned by external authority, it all seems a bit tenuous. It is also true that if, within Anglicanism, the Scriptures are the sole source of doctrines essential for salvation, and if the meaning of Scripture is accessible to all people, it is hardly necessary to resort to a universal gathering, especially since the findings of such a body have already, in advance, been declared to be capable of error.

The position, then, would appear to be that the Anglican Communion cannot determine its doctrine by reference to the decisions of a General Council – whose declarations, like those of Lambeth Conferences, indeed, must therefore be regarded as advisory. Scripture, as an exclusive source of essential doctrine, has become problematical as a consequence of modern Biblical scholarship. The Prayer Book is no longer a standard of order throughout the Communion, or even within constituent Churches, and few, anyway, would any longer consider worship as a means of declaring agreed doctrinal propositions, but more a matter of shared fellowship. So how, in reality, do Anglicans now determine doctrine?

The best test of doctrinal authority is negative, deciding when the Faith is being corrupted. How is error to be recognized? The early Councils of the Church were all called in order to identify heretical ideas. In the Church of England and the Anglican Communion the matter is unclear. The Act of Supremacy in 1534 adhered the *correction* of heresy to the royal prerogative; that does not in itself actually empower the Crown to *determine* what ideas are heretical and what are not, but to deal with heresies that are considered such – or that, at any rate, is how the statute *may* be construed. Perhaps it was also intended that the power should be delegated to a body under ecclesiastical guidance. It is not clear. The difficulty is that the Reformation had cut the English Church off from the canonical authority (the See of Rome) which had before determined heresy, without plainly locating it anywhere. Penalties were provided in the new erastian dispensation, but not the means of identifying the heresy itself. This did not, as it turned out, prevent rival claimants to ortho-doxy from dispatching one another for heresy in the next two centuries, but the problem of defining heresy itself even then related to formulae which dated from the pre-Reformation Church or from the Reformation settlement itself. At first sight it might appear that determining doctrine in the Church of England eventually passed to the jurisdiction of the Judicial Committee of the Privy Council. Until 1832 the court of appeal in doctrinal cases was the High Court of

Delegates, which had succeeded appeal to Rome. In 1832 jurisdiction passed to the Privy Council, a provision which at the time seemed reasonable enough since by then the ecclesiastical courts were almost exclusively taken up with matrimonial and probate cases. Causes with doctrinal implications only very rarely came before them. When, comparatively recently, jurisdiction in doctrinal matters was removed from the Privy Council it was not located elsewhere, so there exists a void at the centre of the issue of who determines erroneous teaching. In the middle of the nineteenth century, however, internal party divisions within the Church of England resulted in a number of cases being heard by the Judicial Committee of the Privy Council, which very publicly highlighted the apparent fact that Anglican doctrine was being determined by a tribunal whose members had no requirement to be – and often were not – members of the Church. The court was also dominated by laymen, and although the Church Discipline Act in 1840 provided for bishops to become members for ecclesiastical causes, many cases, like the Gorham case itself, were not brought under that Act. In 1865 G. C. Broderick and W. H. Freemantle published a volume describing fifteen cases before the Privy Council, between 1840 and 1864, in which the doctrine of the Church of England seemed to have been interpreted. Until the end of the century, as the Colenso case in South Africa showed in 1864, the jurisdiction of the Privy Council in doctrinal matters extended to the Anglican Churches overseas (though never, for obvious reasons, to the Episcopal Church of

America). Yet it is not absolutely clear that the Privy Council, in its deliberations and judgements, was actually *determining* doctrine, despite the overwhelming public perception that this was the case, or whether it managed to keep within the less technical work of seeking to discover what the Church of England's formularies had intended to teach. The Court's proceedings looked like theological constructions because of the often lengthy introduction of theological argument; its decrees commenced with the words, 'In the name of God, Amen.' The problem, as usual, was that the formularies of the Church of England were themselves ambiguous, attempting, as the sixteenth-century theological diversities had seemed to necessitate, comprehensive but imprecise expressions of doctrine. And that meant, in the conditions of nineteenth-century legal enquiry, that extrinsic evidence had sometimes to be heard in order to locate probable original intention. Successive judges in the Judicial Committee were emphatic, however, that their duty was not to determine doctrine as such, but only to apply ecclesiastical law.

It was the Gorham Case in 1850 which brought the difficulty before the public, and which appeared to show that the doctrine of the Church of England – in this case over Baptismal Regeneration – was being determined by a secular tribunal. Lord Langdale, in giving judgement, attempted to adjust understanding of what was happening in his view. The question before them, he said, was not whether Gorham's opinions were 'theologically sound or unsound', but whether they were in correspondence with the formularies of the Church. 'The case not requiring it,' he declared, 'we have abstained from expressing any opinion of our own upon the theological correctness or error of the doctrine held by Mr Gorham which was discussed before us at such length and with so much learning.' It was a conviction frequently expressed by Stephen Lushington, Judge of the High Court of Admiralty and Dean of Arches, and the most distinguished ecclesiastical lawyer of his day, who was involved in all the doctrinal cases which came before the Judicial Committee. 'This is not a court of Divinity,' he said in the *Essays and Reviews* proceedings in 1861, 'it is a court of ecclesiastical law.' In reality, however, law and theological opinion were not so easily separable, and the frequency with which the legal delicacy of Privy Council judges disclaimed their capacity to determine doctrine disguises the fact that for all practical purposes they did so – and were recognized as doing so by the press. Erastian churchmen were untroubled; Tractarians were outraged.

The present void actually seems no inconvenience since the modern Church is not doctrinally contentious – its differences, which are evergreen, relate to matters of order, discipline and moral application. Should the Anglican Communion or the Church of England wish, for example, to contemplate declaring, say, the Assumption of the Virgin as a Doctrine of the Church, there would seem to be no procedure for doing so, and no judicial means of testing the validity of the proceedings. Those who hold to scriptural self-sufficiency will not mind; those who envisage a dynamic function in the magisterium of the Church

will presumably regret the absence of a defining jurisdiction. The matter at the present time seems rather
academic, anyway.

The elimination of a practical procedure for identifying error, and of an accessible appellate jurisdiction
in determining doctrine, have produced a situation in
which Anglicans can only resort to a number of local
provisions, framed in reference to the perceived needs
of the individual member Churches of the Communion, none of which have recognized ultimate authority and none of whom claim it. The resulting
incoherence is usually expressed in terms of paradox:
there is an Anglican rhetoric of self-appraisal in
which chaos is described as order, ambiguity as
richness of comprehension, patent diversity as a
special kind of unity. It has to be said that the
solution of Anglicanism's problem over a Doctrine of
the Church known as 'dispersed authority' is of this
genre. Here, explanation envisages the existence of
mutually conflicting theological beliefs and ecclesiastical orders as a species of creative unity. The pursuit
of institutional comprehensiveness is abandoned, and
the concept of 'the Church' becomes an umbrella
expression providing shelter for an exceedingly
generous range of contentions and panaceas. It was in
Report IV of the Lambeth Conference of 1948 that
'dispersed authority' was first spelled out as a substitute for Anglican ecclesiology – a contribution which
Bishop Sykes, in his acceptance of its leading tenets,
later described as 'the most satisfactory public statement of the Anglican view of authority'. The Lambeth
formula derived, according to its authors, from the

consistent and prolonged 'refusal of a legal basis of union' within the Communion; it depicted 'the positive nature' of Anglican authority as 'moral and spiritual' rather than legal or institutional, and as resting on 'charity'. Its originality lay, in a further Anglican paradox, in its simultaneous espousal of singularity and diversity:

> Authority, as inherited by the Anglican Communion from the undivided Church of the early centuries of the Christian era, is single in that it is derived from a single Divine source, and reflects within itself the richness and historicity of the divine Revelation . . . It is distributed among Scripture, Tradition, Creeds, the Ministry of the Word and Sacraments, the witness of saints, and the *consensus fidelium* . . . It is thus a dispersed rather than a centralized authority having many elements which combine, interact with, and check each other; these elements together contributing by a process of mutual support, mutual checking, and redressing of errors or exaggerations to the many-sided fullness of the authority which Christ has committed to His Church. Where this authority is to be found mediated not in one mode but in several we recognize in this multiplicity God's loving provision against the temptations to tyranny and the dangers of unchecked power.

Moreover the means by which truth is known to be true possess 'a suppleness and elasticity', and a 'quality of richness', which evoke 'a free and willing obedience'. The emphasis on freedom of consent, and the checks and balances within the process, indicate the extent to which this style of explanation is dependent on secular modern concepts of representative and limited government, drawn from the practice of modern democracy. Yet the Report also makes it clear that the consensus of the faithful 'does not depend on mere numbers or on the extension of a belief at any one time, but on continuance through the ages, and the extent to which the consensus is genuinely free'. Without any consciousness of inconsistency the Report also declares that the individual 'Christ-like life carries its own authority'. Here, then is a puzzling mixture. The manner in which doctrine is known to be authentic is dispersed in a fashion which embraces all the variants, individual and collective, which have presented themselves. There is no clue in the Report as to how it is possible to recognize legitimate interpretations from corruptions. What is envisaged is a spiritual free-for-all in which authority is derived from diversity and truth emerges through 'elasticity'. This is rather a frank conclusion. As an account of the ingredients available for a serious discussion of the nature of authority the Report is adequate in its way, at least to the extent that it recognizes the problems. But it offers no prospect of an ordered passage beyond the preliminaries, so that the unitary body of Christ might act in unity. It is easy to forget when reading the Report, that it is not an ecumenical formula – it applies to conditions *inside* the Anglican Churches. Here are, as it were, echoes of Jules Lechevalier's critique of F. D. Maurice: 'Mr Maurice's system is a very good one for bringing men in, but it is all door.'

The Report's insistence on the permanent existence of conflict in the life of the Church is factually accurate. The early Councils were full of rancour. Truth is advanced by the testing of propositions and the questioning of orthodoxies, and periods that are especially characterized by these exercises are creative. The concept of 'dispersed authority', however, does not propose any means of arriving at an orderly conclusion in each particular area of controversy. It is a steady-state; permanent indecision. The more weighty the doctrine at issue the less likely the prospect of a resolution: 'dispersed authority' is a formula for, or rather a description of, the means of reducing Christianity to generalities. The *consensus fidelium* , it is true, is very properly *not* defined as a majority in the Report – it does 'not depend on mere numbers'. But it is only one of several means by which doctrine is to be recognized as authentic; it is explicitly linked to conciliar decisions and these, in turn, are described as resting only 'at least in part' on 'their acceptance by the whole body of the faithful'. Even this dimension of the process can hardly be organic or dynamic, since Anglican ecclesiology also incorporates the notion that Councils are capable of error in fundamentals, and that without the consent of the political order they cannot even be summoned. Bishop Sykes, in his *Integrity of Anglicanism* (1978), rightly regards conflict in the identification of doctrine as unavoidable, and sees the 'Anglican history of the experience of conflict' as 'of potentially great service'. What he also says, however, in amplification of the Lambeth report of 1948, is that 'authentic Christian preaching and living can only be achieved in the midst of ambiguity'. Why is that so? The Catholic Church has a clear record of perpetual examination and re-examination of doctrine, tremendous internal controversy, but an ability to arrive at precise formulations. Anglicans are sceptical of this, both because they disapprove of some of the doctrinal decisions achieved in this way, and of the procedure itself – presumably what the Report of 1948 implied when it referred to 'tyranny'. Sykes believes that *all* Christian formulations of doctrine 'will be necessarily controversial', and observes that 'there will be no certainty that the decision made as a result of the conflict will be correct'. Authority, he concludes, cannot be 'embodied' in institutions; there is only a 'continuous process involving all the participators' of discussion and exploration. Despite the distinction of this analysis it remains descriptive; authority is a latency, not a fixed reality. And how very modern it is: a process for arguing about belief derived from committee culture and the participation born of mass education. It would have been impossible to apply this understanding of 'dispersed authority' in preceding centuries. It may be impossible to apply now. As for the positive advantages of the unavoidable existence of conflict – how far that is from the sensibilities of the modern Anglican leadership, who are horrified by controversy. Lambeth Conferences have arguably been preoccupied more with the prevention of controversy than with constructive or prophetic advance. There is, at any rate, the authority of Hooker, no less, for the priority of error over controversy – it was better, he wrote, 'that sometime an erroneous sentence definitive should prevail, till the same authority perceiving such oversight, might afterwards correct or reverse it, than that strifes should have respite to grow'.

The most telling difficulty about 'dispersed authority' is that four centuries of its operation in the Church of England has produced what most acknowledge: a crisis of identity, a crisis of unity, and an inability to adduce a coherent ecclesiology. It is hard to imagine that divine providence, disclosed in the guidance of the Holy Spirit, can have entrusted the presence of Christ in the world to such an ideological shambles. So the search for an Anglican Doctrine of the Church must resume; 'dispersed authority' is not satisfactory. In entrusting himself, not to a philosophy but to an organic people, Christ remained indivisibly a person – not a wide and dispersed range of inclinations. It is scarcely conceivable that a person should only be known about *via* a tortuous dialectic of truth alternating with error, and remain, still, identifiable through centuries of belief. The simple fact is also that at the time of the Reformation the question of an independent ecclesiology was not resolved when an independent Church was being set up.

Now some will say that this is all a matter of technicalities, that Anglicans have in practice retained the essential doctrines of Christianity in an orthodox form despite the apparent absence of an agreed method of defining doctrine. Some will say this because they still regard Scriptural self-sufficiency as obviating the need for enquiry at all, and some because the external episcopal governance of Anglicanism corresponds to historic models and has passed the test of preserving orthodoxy. Many will declare that much teaching in the Church of England today, as heard in the pulpit, or as falls from the lips of ecclesiastical dignitaries, is very far from orthodox. From a Catholic perspective, additionally, it can be pointed out that the absence of a dynamic means of determining doctrine has resulted in the Anglicans' inability to develop belief – for example relating to the place of the Virgin in the redemptive scheme. Many will doubtless be relieved that that is so. Yet Anglicanism has unquestionably lived off the fat of pre-Reformation accumulations and has, since the sixteenth century, been in a kind of doctrinal limbo. A Doctrine of the Church *is* required. Christianity has until now existed within the general parameters of Hellenistic-Latin culture, which may not prove so durable in the future. Perhaps we are still in the early days of the Church – taking a long perspective into the unknowable future. Perhaps it is near its end, with the end of all things. There is no way of telling. It is unlikely, however, that the main concepts of the Mediterranean cultures which have determined the development of Christ's revelation will persist forever, and the Church will then need to bring forth treasures new and old in a much more radical fashion, calculated according to the terms available in future arrangements of human knowledge. The means by which truth is known to be true, the question of authority in teaching, will then be absolutely crucial. This is not a problem for the historic Churches, which have dynamic Doctrines of the Church. But Anglicans have a real issue to address. The basic division remains: do Christians have access to an infallible teaching office, as the historic Churches have always claimed, or are the Protestants right in supposing that only Scripture is indefectible? There is no *Via Media* here – Anglicans in this bleak assessment are thoroughly Protestant. In the future, as in the past, the matter of what, in the political sphere, used to be called 'entryism' will be a major threat to the integrity of religious institutions. Alien ideology and secular moral orthodoxy may identify themselves with Christian ethical teaching, and there will be those inside the Churches who may, correspondingly, associate basic Christianity with various enthusiasms for humanity. The ancient problem of heresy, therefore remains: how to distinguish truth from error, how to protect received teachings from corruptions, and how not to depart from the mind of Christ when determining doctrinal formulations. There is little in the human record so far to suggest that it is possessed of self-correcting mechanisms, and that somehow truth will inevitably emerge in a recognizable form. The Church of Christ embodies Christ; there are unitary consequences for the way Christians therefore conduct themselves institutionally if truth is not only to be determined but to be transmitted. A Doctrine of the Church is unavoidable, and the Church of England may well be approaching the conjunction of a crisis of identity and a general cultural crisis, so that it will be obliged to address the problem with greater clarity than in the past. It has not got much time left to address the problem before it is, anyway, overtaken by its other internal sicknesses.

9

Does the Church of England have a future?

❦

Institutions have a way of lasting much longer than their social utility would suggest likely – sometimes for decades, or even centuries. This country offers many examples of ancient charities and corporate bodies which have long outlived their real purposes, and now enjoy a quaint existence undisturbed by noticeable function, except, perhaps, to small groups of involved enthusiasts or chance beneficiaries. The Church of England is in line to join them. It has been ailing for many years, but as its sickness becomes more critical, an acceleration in the dissolution of its vitality can be expected. But actual death is unlikely: a rump will survive. It can probably look to a future comparable to the condition of Orthodox Christianity in modern Turkey, where the Patriarch of Constantinople survives, living modestly in a suburb of Istanbul, his former cathedral a state museum. For as far as it is possible to predict, there will always be an Archbishop of Canterbury, and bishops – probably more in number than their usefulness should indicate, since, guided by the example of the cults which died at the end of the ancient world, when ceremonial became more florid, and official titles were more freely handed out, it is to be expected that bishops will multiply as parish priests decline. The institutional husks of the Church of England persist, propped up by the survival of centralized finance. The Church Commissioners, that is to say, are the one really efficient part of ecclesiastical machinery – and they, due to the nature of the Establishment of religion, are civil servants. The position would look very different if the connection of Church and State was ever severed, for then the re-endowment of the disestablished Church, following the precedent set by Ireland in 1869, would leave the Church administered (from whatever modest buildings the C. of E. would flee to) by church officials themselves. Inefficiency and the postponement of necessary decisions could then be safely predicted. So the extent to which the material husks can keep the plant standing upright must be posited as a matter only of conjecture. And it is a support relating merely to clerical stipends and the maintenance of some other financial benefits transferred to Crown administration after the nineteenth century reforms of the Church, which began in the 1830s. An institution which has already outlived its purpose, judged according to public use of its services, and intellectual endorsement of its authority, can only go on until it collapses in upon itself – until the husks fall away.

For an assessment of that possibility the observer should consider the state of the parishes. Parochial ministry has been thought to be Anglicanism *par excellence*; the heart of the whole enterprise, what the husks exist to protect – the filling. But it is all rotting anyway. Changes in the nature of society itself have made the antiquated parochial units unable to identify suitable constituents to address. Social mobility, the privatization of modern family life, the loss of a close relationship between the place of work and the location of residence, the decline of voluntary associations which formerly socialized children and prepared them for membership of religious bodies, the recession of social discipline and of respect for local leaders, and especially for vicars, the capability of personal transport to widen the possibilities for leisure and to provide even the remaining church-goers with the means of choice in worship, the removal of social functions from the parish to the secular social services, the arrival, with television, and now of the internet, of a means of acquiring informed opinion without the need of ecclesiastical agents, the sheer disinclination of a population satiated with material pleasures to attend a sermon delivered by a minister who probably gets his knowledge from the same vehicles of public debate as they do themselves: all these conspire to render the Anglican parish redundant. The noble ideal of the priest, the familiar repository of historical memory, the fading after-glow of the world we have lost: the parish unit is heavily romanticized – especially inside the Church – and rarely used. The ancient territorial ideal was a good one; with a national Church, everyone could reside within the pastoral responsibility of an incumbent priest, and so be able to call upon the ministrations of religion.

The reality today, however, is of tiny gatherings of people in largely empty buildings, offering worship which they have selected themselves from the new service-books – which is unknown to the wider public, and even to other Christians in the same Church of England – and who are quite unrepresentative of society immediately around them. Their bond of union is social class; there are very few congregations which have a significantly large working-class membership. There is also a disturbing impression of a certain oddity. There is every good reason why the Church should be the refuge of those who do not fit into society, or of the mentally disturbed: here is a proper ministry, an essential dimension of Christian service and an authentic presence of the Lord. But when the numbers of those supporting an institution begin to exhibit a disproportionately high incidence of social maladjustment there should be warning signals. The last devotees who visited the sanctuaries of Greece in the third century were thought to be a bit weird.

Yet the parish continues to be the essential ideal of Christian ministry in the modern Church of England. The leaders have no other strategy to secure a religious presence, no further vision then the style and form they have known all their lives. Their idea of reform is an adjustment of the *status quo*; a regrouping of parishes, a consolidation of ministerial resources, and, finally, in a burst of apparent and much-paraded modernity, the use by the parish priests of electronic means of communication in those places where their flocks have the appropriate devices of response. There are periodic discussions about new types of ministerial training, but again, these tend to centre upon structures rather than content: the proposals for change do not seem to envisage any significant departure from the existing courses – which bear affinity to the liberal-arts approaches found in secular higher education. And now that the bishops are largely drawn from the ranks of the parish priests, and lack knowledge of the rapidly changing world of affairs around them, their inherent institutional conservatism, and the consequent dogged adhesion to the parochial structure, is actually growing. The deans of cathedrals, similarly, are now usually chosen on the basis of their managerial expertise; they too, have very little in the way of an alternative context in which to assess the future of the Church beyond the immediate boundaries. They see their cathedrals as grand parish churches and, under the pressure of funding crises, heritage assets.

The financial difficulties of the cathedrals, in fact, are not the worst of their troubles, though they are usually the most visible. They are being depressed and secularized under the weight of regulation. For a decade, now, the Fabric Advisory Committees – statutory bodies of which the Chapters are not members – have gained effective control of the maintenance of the buildings, stipulating, though not funding, the nature of necessary works. They are gradually extending their remit, which originally applied only to fixed fabric, to all kinds of furnishings and artefacts. The Chapters have also to meet the requirements of Health and Safety legislation, Disabled

Access, fire rules: all require the installation of devices which need permanent monitoring or attention, and the expense of employing staff competent to oversee the administration of the necessary obligations. English Heritage sets guidelines as to what the cathedrals may do with their buildings, and since their rulings sometimes appear to conflict with the legal requirement of other statutory bodies – Disabled Access, for example – a good deal of overlapping jurisdiction is leading to confusion and uncertainty. The point, however, is that the cathedral clergy, and their lay canons, are subject to much regulation, and only in the conduct of the worship itself do they still enjoy autonomy – under the scrutiny of internal regulation provided, if necessary, by the Cathedral Council. The cathedrals are often considered an exception to the general decline of the Church, but it is not really so. Their enlarged congregations are a sign of dissatisfaction with parish worship by those who remove themselves. Visitors and tourists attend the services of cathedrals because they like the music. The hard-core congregations are really very modest in size, and are likely to decline sharply when the age-profile of those fleeing the parish churches necessarily diminishes the supply. On present showing the pot will empty in about ten years. Another problem for the cathedrals is that the heritage industry in general is in decline, and the numbers of those for whom a visit to a cathedral satisfies a taste for gothic quaintness is diminishing. As they become fewer the financial burden on the cathedral authorities has to be borne from alternative resources. Only a minority of the cathedrals are sufficiently well known to be able to meet the shortfall in their finances by floating an appeal or making the public pay to enter the church. It is getting impossible to avoid the conclusion that these great buildings will, in a decade or two, be administered by some agency of the State. The Church of England cannot afford them.

In the parishes the financial problems are even more pressing. To express it extremely simply: when the congregations decline numerically to a certain level they can no longer raise enough money to keep the roof on. Like the cathedrals, they receive no grants of public money, though, again like the cathedrals, some of them have endowments of their own. These private sources of income are proving wholly inadequate to meet the modern costs of maintaining a building, especially an historic one, now that statutory regulation requires such exacting standards. Increasingly, also, parishes are unable to meet their 'quota' – a payment made to the diocese to defray central costs, so the dioceses, too, exist in a state of chronic financial crisis. The entire parochial system will break down in a decade or so, and with it will go the only model of ecclesiastical polity the Church leaders have to hand. Presumably a radical re-grouping of individual congregations will remain a permanent phenomenon of Anglicanism, and the result will be a small number of operating churches existing at the social margin. It is difficult to see how any new members can be recruited. The Church schools have patently failed over the past thirty years – since the liberals ruined their confessional basis –

to provide new members. The chaplaincies in higher education define themselves as though they were adjuncts of the secular social services; and when it comes to the presentation of Christianity their liberal agenda will not allow anything other than an 'open-ended' approach to the message they are employed to convey. The population generally want to make up the content of religious belief for themselves – in the small amount of space allocated in their lives even to this enterprise – and do not usually look to the Church for guidance. Those who do associate their version of Christianity with the sort of thing upheld in the Churches sometimes attend services for a while, only to fall away when they discover that what is on offer is not in correspondence with their own inventions. This may not be an age of irreligion indeed, but an age in which people simply regard themselves as capable of arriving at religious ideas without resorting to existing traditions and institutions. In view of the vagueness and ambiguity of what many Anglican clergy propagate, it is in some ways surprising that the Church cannot find a home for modern enquirers after truth. Making up the content of religion for oneself, after all, is what the Anglican clergy have been doing for centuries.

There is one area in which the Churches, and especially the Church of England, do retain some connection with social need: the rites of passage. Here, too, however, the present time witnesses a decline which shows every sign of deepening rapidly. Fewer and fewer children are being baptized, and this is not being compensated by adult baptisms. Parents either no longer respect the means by which people are admitted to membership of the Church, or do not consider a formal entry necessary, or, most likely, simply no longer live in a culture in which the need for baptism naturally occurs as an accompaniment of childbirth. Weddings are increasingly celebrated in secular venues, which the participants consider beautiful or convenient. Clergy are familiar with appeals made by supplicants for a church ceremony who have no real association with the life of the parish; these, anyway, are declining as the taste for secular events increases. Funerals remain the most frequent occasion when the clergy have any spiritual connection with the unchurched. These, too, however, are not as common as might seem likely; chaplains at crematoria take most of the services, and there is then no liaison with the parish or its minister. Actual secular funeral rites are increasing. Formerly they were largely the choice of intellectuals and professional-class people, where detachment from religion in life had been a matter of conscious choice rather than lost habit; today they are increasingly chosen by people in all parts of society who have had no attendance at a church in their lifetime, or whose surviving relatives make the same judgement on their behalf. It is now very common, especially in middle-class funerals, for the relatives to seek to make up the form of service for themselves – leaving the hapless priest to carry out their selection of moving poems and music the deceased particularly favoured. Thus even funerals no longer always embody a uniform or distinct Christian teaching, but are personalized composites reflecting the emotional preferences of relatives. The rites of passage are, in fact, no longer an important means by which the Church of England can establish links with those outside the Church. They may, however, point to the possible future use of a number of churches and cathedrals – as the venues of secular weddings and funerals, halls for the performance of ritualized but religionless ceremonies.

It is now usual for the Evangelicals in the Church of England to indicate the success of Evangelical Churches as evidence that decline is not inevitable, and that the future lies with them. This seems an extremely unlikely prognosis. Evangelicalism is, in itself, an insecure basis for a Church which has national coherence. To many, it appears an intellectually unsophisticated understanding of Christianity, and its central tenet – that individuals receive direct intimations of the divine presence – unlikely. That the emotional intimacy of most Evangelical worship should appeal to a society of increasing educational accomplishment is also an unsure calculation. It has a certain appeal as a folk religion, and attracts a modest educated fringe at the present time; there is little to sustain a continued adhesion of the latter in the long term, however. The statistics of Evangelical increase are insubstantial, and many of those younger people who join Evangelical congregations give up after a relatively short period, often because they change the location of their residence and cannot find a satisfactory place for sympathetic worship in their new district. Evangelicals reap the same poor harvest as the other groups in the Church when it comes to the fragility of self-selected religious opinions and emotionally preferred worship. The decline of attendance at the mainstream Evangelical churches in the United States in the last thirty years is the writing on the wall. Evangelicals make much of the new electronic churches in America, and the 'mega-church' phenomenon; both, however, have done little in statistical terms to compensate for the leeching away of the attendances at the Churches of the conventional denominations.

The Roman Catholic Church in England is experiencing the same pattern of decline as the Church of England, but it is a little further down the road, due to the more substantial basis from which the decline is taking place. And above all, of course, the Catholic Church does not have, at least in its direction from Rome, the same problems of ideological incoherence, at the very centre of its existence, from which Anglicanism suffers. From European countries and from North America, of course, liberals are baying away at the gates of the Vatican, and demanding a relaxation both of doctrinal precision and moral discipline. English Roman Catholics have contracted the Protestant virus, and it will prove as destructive to their body as it has among the Anglicans. But the Catholics are offshoots of a plant which has authentically global roots, and its vitality is plainly evident from many of them. The future of the Church seems to be entrusted to the southern hemisphere, and its orthodoxy of teaching is guaranteed for so long as Rome itself retains centralized authority. The Anglican Communion, in contrast, is nothing more than a periodic conference of once like-minded individual Churches who have little in common now, but a colonial past.

Will the Church of England survive? Something called the Church of England is likely to continue. Anglicanism is so ideologically insubstantial that it is capable of incorporating seemingly any set of ideas. Its doctrinal basis remains orthodox, but it does not act as if one exists, and it certainly makes no impact in its friable attempts at religious teaching. Riddled with liberalism, and therefore unable to speak authoritatively on many issues – having relativized the means by which it can recognize truth – the Church staggers on to a modest and confined future. With each internal crisis its stature is diminished; its presence in society becomes more obscured by the flying debris of minor conflict. Its fancy-dress presence at national events disguises its absence in the affections of the people. There was, until quite recently, a residual attachment to the Church of England: it was an undemanding but familiar presence, called into existence at times of family need or family crisis. Now it is becoming the subject even of subdued amusement – to many an irrelevance in a society which ignores it when seeking moral guidance or moral clarity. The infrastructure of the Church will surely collapse; the surviving marginalized clergy, wrapped, still, in the ceremonial attire once hallowed by historical resonance, will be there, in small numbers, mostly unnoticed. At the edge of society they will seek a function or a purpose with the same admirable tenacity that they have always shown.